CREATING Keepsakes

SCRAPBOOK | **MAGAZINE**

A TREASURY OF FAVORITES

SCRAPBOOKING
SOLUTIONS

Presenting over 850 of the best designs and ideas
from *Creating Keepsakes* publications, to solve scrapbooking
challenges in organization, creativity, photography, and technology.

PRODUCED EXCLUSIVELY FOR LEISURE ARTS

Founding Editor	Lisa Bearnson
Co-founder	Don Lambson
Editor-in-Chief	Tracy White
Special Projects Editor	Leslie Miller
Copy Editor	Kim Sandoval
Editorial Assistants	Joannie McBride, Fred Brewer
Administrative Assistant	Michelle Bradshaw
Art Director	Brian Tippetts
Designer	Blue Sky Studios
Production Designers	Just Scan Me!, Exposure Graphics
Publisher	Mark Seastrand
Media Relations	Alicia Bremer, 801/364-2030
Web Site Manager	Emily Johnson
Assistant Web Site Editor	Sarah Wilcox
Production Manager	Gary Whitehead
Business Sales Manager	Tara Schofield
Business Sales Assistants	Jacque Jensen, Melanie Cain
Advertising Sales Manager	Becky Lowder
Wholesale Accounts	800/815-3538

Donna Hair, stores A–G,
and outside of U.S., ext. 235

Victoria James, stores H–R, ext. 226

Kristin Schaefer, stores S–Z
(except "Scr"), ext. 250

Sherrie Burt, stores starting with "Scr,"
ext. 244

Kim Biehn, distributor accounts, ext. 251

PRIMEDIA
Consumer Magazine & Internet Group

Vice President, Group Publisher	David O'Neil
Circulation Director	Lisa Harris
Associate Circulation Director	Darcy Cruwys
Circulation Manager	Sara Gunn
Promotions Manager	Stephanie Michas
Business Manager	Laurie Halvorsen

PRIMEDIA, Inc.

Chairman	Dean Nelson
President & CEO	Kelly Conlin
Vice-Chairman	Beverly C. Chell

PRIMEDIA Enthusiast Media

EVP Consumer Marketing/Circulation	Steve Aster
SVP/Chief Financial Officer	Kevin Neary
SVP, Mfg., Production & Distribution	Kevin Mullan
SVP/Chief Information Officer	Debra C. Robinson
VP, Consumer Marketing	Bobbi Gutman
VP, Manufacturing	Gregory A. Catsaros
VP, Single Copy Sales	Thomas L. Fogarty
VP, Manufacturing Budgets & Operations	Lilia Golia
VP, Human Resources	Kathleen P. Malinowski
VP, Business Development	Albert Messina
VP, Database / e-Commerce	Suti Prakash

PRIMEDIA Outdoor Recreation and Enthusiast Group

SVP, Group Publishing Director	Brent Diamond
SVP, Marketing and Internet Operations	Stephen H. Bender
VP, Marketing and Internet Operations	Dave Evans

SUBSCRIPTIONS

To subscribe to *Creating Keepsakes* magazine or to change the address of your current subscription, call or write:

Phone: 888/247-5282
International: 760/745-2809
Fax: 760/745-7200

Subscriber Services
Creating Keepsakes
P.O. Box 469007
Escondido, CA 92046-9007

Some back issues of *Creating Keepsakes* magazine are available for $5 each, payable in advance.

NOTICE OF LIABILITY

The information in this book is distributed on an "as is" basis, without warranty. While every precaution has been taken in the preparation of this book, neither the author nor PRIMEDIA Inc. nor LEISURE ARTS Inc. shall have any liability to any person or entity with respect to any liability, loss or damage caused or alleged to be caused directly or indirectly by the instructions contained in this book.

TRADEMARKS

Trademarked names are used throughout this book. Rather than put a trademark symbol in every occurrence of a trademarked name, we state we are using the names only in an editorial fashion and to the benefit of the trademark owner with no intention of infringement of the trademark.

CORPORATE OFFICES

Creating Keepsakes is located at 14901 Heritagecrest Way, Bluffdale, UT 84065. Phone: 801/984-2070. Fax: 801/984-2080. Home page: *www.creatingkeepsakes.com*.

Scrapbooking Solutions
Hardcover ISBN 1-57486-458-0
Softcover ISBN 1-57486-459-9
Library of Congress Control Number 2004113012

Published by Leisure Arts, Inc., 5701 Ranch Drive, Little Rock, Arkansas 72223. 501-868-8800. *www.leisurearts.com*. Printed in the United States of America.

Special Projects Director: Susan Frantz Wiles
Vice President and Editor-in-Chief: Sandra Graham Case
Executive Director of Publications: Cheryl Nodine Gunnells
Senior Publications Director: Susan White Sullivan
Senior Design Director: Cyndi Hansen
Senior Art Operations Director: Jeff Curtis
Art Imaging Director: Mark Hawkins
Director of Retail Marketing: Stephen Wilson
Director of Designer Relations: Debra Nettles
Graphic Design Supervisor: Amy Vaughn
Graphic Artist: Katherine Atchison
Associate Editor: Susan McManus Johnson
Editorial Assistants: JoAnn Forrest, Merrilee Gasaway, Amy Hansen, April Hansen, and Janie Wright
Imaging Technicians: Stephanie Johnson and Mark Potter
Publishing Systems Administrator: Becky Riddle
Publishing Systems Assistants: Clint Hanson, John Rose, and Chris Wertenberger

Publisher: Rick Barton
Vice President, Finance: Tom Siebenmorgen
Director of Corporate Planning and Development: Laticia Mull Dittrich
Vice President, Retail Marketing: Bob Humphrey
Vice President, Sales: Ray Shelgosh
Vice President, National Accounts: Pam Stebbins
Director of Sales and Services: Margaret Reinold
Vice President, Operations: Jim Dittrich
Comptroller, Operations: Rob Thieme
Retail Customer Service Manager: Stan Raynor
Print Production Manager: Fred F. Pruss

Our Favorite Solutions for Your Scrapbooks

In our *Creating Keepsakes* editorial team meetings, we are constantly concerned with one thing: Are we providing our readers with solutions for their scrapbooking challenges? Every month within the pages of *Creating Keepsakes* you'll find that our editors and contributors have searched the industry far and wide, as well as looking in some not-so-expected places, in order to give you fresh, helpful solutions.

That's why I'm so excited to offer this volume. Here we've gathered some of our best solutions from the past two years of *Creating Keepsakes* magazine. These scrapbooking solutions will make scrapbooking easier, more fun, and an all around great experience. From organization to creativity to technology, you'll find solutions to most of your scrapbooking challenges inside this volume. I know that this is one book I'll reach for over and over again—and I'm sure you will too. ❤

Happy Scrapping!

Tracy

Editor-in-Chief
Creating Keepsakes Magazine

JODEE MADDER

185

KIMBERLY KWON

104

contents

SCRAPBOOKING SOLUTIONS

10

120

Supply Solutions

Photography and Technology Solutions

71

172

MISSION: Organization

A formula for success—no matter how much stuff you have

by Becky Higgins • Photography by Roger Mastroianni

Ask anyone who knows me well, and they'll tell you I love to organize. As a young girl, I organized my brothers' bedrooms and created neighborhood clubs. As a teenager, I made lists and charts. They documented my homework, the people I exchanged school pictures with, and what I wanted to pack for summer camp. (Am I really telling you this?)

As an adult, I've planned and organized more baby showers, youth events and parties than I can even recall. Organization is in my blood—I couldn't deny it if I tried.

Although this mania is a running theme throughout my life, it wasn't until I watched the Oprah Winfrey TV show that I had an "a-ha!" moment. Oprah's guest that day was Julie Morgenstern, a professional organizer, speaker, and author of *Time Management from the Inside Out* and *Organizing from the Inside Out*. Julie shared her organization formula, which applies to virtually anything, including your hobby space.

Here is my interpretation of Julie's advice, specific to organizing your scrapbooking items. Whether you have one corner in a room or an entire room dedicated to your hobby, these concepts will help you organize *anything*.

Formula for Organizing

S – Sort
P – Purge
A – Assign
C – Containerize
E – Equalize

Sort

The first step is to identify what's important to you, then group similar items (top left). You'll likely need a lot of floor space to spread everything out. Next, group items in the way that will best meet your needs. If you decide to group by category, for example, gather eyelets in one pile and tags in another.

Continue sorting within the groups if desired. You can sort your scraps into different colors (middle); you can even combine groups after everything is divided. Decide what will work best for you.

Purge

Decide what you can live without and get rid of it. Let's face it—if you're hanging on to motorcycle stickers you *might* need one day, let go, my friend. They're like the size 4 skirt from 1993 that probably won't ever fit again. It's OK to let go. Remember, you're making room for fun new products.

Everything you purge goes somewhere. Some of it may be trash, and that's where it belongs. If you have kids who like art projects, put unwanted supplies in a bin for them. It'll keep them out of your most expensive supplies, plus you're encouraging your kids to be creative and value scrapbooking. Don't forget to give them extra pictures to work with, too.

Other items can probably be donated (bottom left). When I come across something I know I won't use, it goes in my give-away box. Remember: one scrapbooker's trash is another's treasure. Share with your friends or organize a swap with cropping buddies. You can also donate unwanted items to local schools and shelters.

Assign

Decide where to store your supplies. Julie Morgenstern reminds us to make sure the location is logical, accessible and safe. If you work in a closet, decide what stays on the table and what's stored elsewhere. If you have an entire scrapbooking room, include everyday supplies in the area where you scrapbook. Your infrequently used items can go on the other side of the room.

Top left: Group your supplies into categories. **Middle:** Sort supplies by color, texture, size and more. **Bottom:** Donate unwanted supplies to friends, schools and shelters.

Take the S.P.A.C.E. Challenge

January is a new year and a fresh beginning. Make it a successful scrapbooking year by getting organized. You may choose to do this in a weekend or work on it for five hours a week in January. Don't delay—you'll love having everything in its place.

Need a little help tackling your scrapbooking space? Enlist the help of your friends. Keep tabs on each other as you make progress and offer support and suggestions along the way.

My working space is in a closet in my office (top right). I keep my adhesive, scissors, eyelet-setting kit and most-used pens in a handy spot beside my paper trimmer. I use these items almost every time I work on a scrapbook page or card. My totes of extra photos are on the other side of my room because I don't refer to them as often.

Work with your available space. Adjacent to my closet is an old, exposed brick wall, window and my big, red chair (opposite left). I knew this would be a great spot to install a grid unit for my totes. Decide where you want to house your supplies and tools based on how often you use them.

Containerize

This is the fun part! Now that you know where your supplies will go, make sure everything has a home, whether it's a drawer, tote, plastic container, binder or basket (bottom). Your containers should be sturdy, easy to handle and the right size. (It doesn't hurt to have them look good, too.) Watch for options online or at your local scrapbook store.

Says Julie, "The art of containerizing is to do it last, not first." I often jump the gun and containerize before I sort. Inevitably, I find I still need something later when I sort. Save yourself the hassle and follow Julie's suggested order.

Once everything is containerized, put your containers in their predetermined places. Step back, enjoy the satisfaction of completing a huge task, and reward yourself with a big milkshake. (See, I told you that size 4 skirt wasn't worth hanging on to!)

Equalize

Spend 15 minutes each day maintaining what you've organized. If you spend a little time putting things away after making a big mess, you'll easily keep your space organized. After all, isn't this what you teach your kids about their rooms?

Final Thoughts

The key to making this formula work? Follow the steps in order. When things are organized and I know where to find everything, I'm not only more efficient, but I feel more creative. I hope this formula helps you get your own scrapbooking space organized. Thanks, Julie!

Opposite: A grid unit works well to organize your containers.
Top: Keep your most frequently used supplies within easy reach.
Bottom left: De-clutter your space by storing supplies in drawers.
Bottom right: Create a filing system for paper scraps.

Brighten Up Your Workspace
Products that'll shed a little light

by Rachel Thomae

Now that you've got your scrapbook area organized, it's time to brighten up your workspace. The following lighting options will help you see your layouts in a whole new light!

Ultralux Floor Lamp

Don't have room for a desk lamp? Try a floor lamp instead! Ultralux's natural-light floor lamp features a flexible arm so you can position your light source in your scrap area.

Web site: www.fullspectrumsolutions.com
Phone: 888/574-7014

Daylight Scrapbooker's Lamp

Designed expressly for scrapbookers, the Daylight Scrapbooker's Lamp includes a low-heat, daylight simulation bulb for accurate color matching and reduced eyestrain. The removable "tidy tray" let you store your favorite scrapbooking tools within easy reach.

Web site: www.daylightcompany.com
Phone: 866/329-5444

Mighty Bright Craft Light

Looking for a portable option? The compact Mighty Bright Craft Light can be clipped to a table or a shelf. It can also be used as a freestanding light—great for providing extra light at crops. An optional magnifying accessory is also available.

Web site: www.goldcrestinc.com
Phone: 800/922-3233

Like what you see in Becky's room?

Here is where you can find many of the items.

Kokuyo • Organizational totes
(*Note:* Available in four colors)
Phone: 877/465-6589
E-mail: *info@kokuyo-usa.com*
Check your local scrapbook store
or visit *www.scrapbooks.com*.

Display Dynamics • Stacking trays
for 12" x 12" paper
Phone: 732/356-1961 ext. 122
Web site: *www.displaydynamics.net*
Check your local craft or scrapbook store.
(*Note:* You can find trays for 8½" x 11"
paper at most office supply stores.)

Novelcrafts • Wire paper racks for
12" x 12" paper
Phone: 541/582-3208
Web site: *www.novelcrafts.com*
(*Note:* Check out *www.westendwire.com*
for other options.)

ArtBin by Flambeau, Inc. • Clear boxes
Phone: 800/232-3474
Web site: *www.artbin.com*
Check your local craft or scrapbook store.

Display Dynamics • Two-drawer
mobile cabinet
Phone: 732/356-1961 x122
Web site: *www.displaydynamics.net*
Check your local craft or scrapbook store.

Cropper Hopper by Leeco • Hanging
file folders
Phone: 800/826-8806
Web site: *www.cropperhopper.com*
Check your local craft or scrapbook store.

Linens-n-Things • Metal mesh grid unit
Phone: 866/568-7378
Web site: *www.lnt.com*

EK Success • Pen cases
Web site: *www.eksuccess.com*
Check your local craft or
scrapbook store.

Longaberger • Baskets
Phone: 800/966-0374
Web site: *www.longaberger.com*

Sterilite • See-through drawer units
E-mail: *custsrvc@sterilite.com*
Web site: *www.sterilite.com*
Check your local discount, hardware, office
supply, craft or drug store. ❤

creating
spaces

ORGANIZE YOUR SCRAPBOOKING SUPPLIES

MEET GAIL. MEET GAIL'S CLOSET.

Meet Gail's pile of scrapbook supplies in the corner of her dining room. No, this isn't a TV show—this is real life! No crew to magically solve problems. No carpenter to build storage units on a moment's notice. And a real-life budget to accomplish the project!

Readers loved Becky Higgins' ideas and scrapbooking closet in "Mission: Organization". Many asked for help creating their own scrapbooking space. So we called Gail Robinson, an avid scrapbooker, to see if we could organize a space for her. She was excited! To make the closet a "real world" solution that most readers could afford, we limited the project's cost to $200 or less.

Before

by patti coombs

After

More before shots:

Gail's closet (left) couldn't hold all her scrapbooking supplies when we started.

Gail's scrapbooking cart (above) was stored in the corner of her dining room.

TIP: Sketch out your ideas and take measurements before shopping for storage solutions.

Getting Started

I met with Gail to view her current setup (see photos above). Her three main problems? Lack of shelf space, odd angles in the ends of the closet, and the fact that most of her scrapbooking supplies were not even in the closet.

Next, I asked lots of questions to determine what Gail wanted. Her three main goals were:

- more accessible paper
- better fiber storage
- more organized paper scraps

Gail wanted to store sewing and craft supplies in the same closet, and she didn't want to do anything that couldn't be removed later if needed.

By determining first what Gail wanted to achieve, we were able to make decisions as we went along that helped her reach her goals. (See "My Closet Makeover" on page 21.) We decided what would be stored in the closet, then began gathering the supplies into one place.

patti's expanded formula

In "Mission: Organiziation", Becky Higgins introduced you to Julie Morgenstern's organizing methods. Following are my additions to the formula:

Space   Utilization: Define what you want to accomplish so you'll end up with the desired results. Stand back and evaluate what you've got. Gather everything to a single spot. Sort into categories that work for you.

Purge   Be selective! Prioritize: Determine what you use most often.

Assess   your home base. Decide what you need most. More shelves? More drawers? Assign a home. Place your most-used items in the most accessible area.

Creative containerizing   Check into other types of containers (fishing, sewing, office supply and more). Childproofing and other considerations: Do you need a door that locks? Are you right- or left-handed? Are your supplies extremely heavy?

Evaluate   Stand back and check. Are you meeting your goals? Enjoy! Have fun scrapbooking with your organized supplies. Equalize: Take the time to KEEP organized.

Along the Way

I taught Gail the following concepts as we worked on coming up with organizational solutions:

Categorize: Sort your tools and supplies into categories. Subdivide any category that becomes unmanageable. We sorted Gail's items into 17 categories: cutting tools, punches, stamping supplies, templates and rulers, photos, memorabilia, embellishments, tools, scraps, stickers and die cuts, chalks and paints, miscellaneous doodads, fibers, pens and pencils, page protectors, paper and adhesives.

I like to subdivide my paper supply into three categories. First, I separate paper by size (8½" x 11" and 12" x 12"). Next I separate by type of paper (such as patterned, cardstock, vellum or handmade), then by color or design.

Group: Group items according to the way your brain works. I generally use my stamping ink like chalk, so I store my ink pads with my chalks instead of my stamps. We stored Gail's walnut ink and chalk together.

Purge: Get rid of anything that doesn't work, is broken or that you don't enjoy using. Create a pile of items that belong elsewhere. Return them to their homes later so you don't get sidetracked now.

Be realistic about what you will actually use and recycle the rest. I donate my extra supplies to a local children's hospital.

Choose sturdy, durable shelving and containers for long-term storage.

TIP: Purchase organizers made of heavier plastic or acrylic so they'll hold up over time. I love the Optimizers by Rubbermaid.

Convert a kitchen utensils caddy into a container for oft-used items.

Prioritize: Identify which items you use most often and store them where they're most accessible. The same goes for photos you're currently scrapbooking.

Gail and I converted a kitchen utensils caddy into a "basics" box full of items she uses often (see above right). This container holds Gail's favorite pair of scissors, pens, adhesives, a ruler, some paint brushes and a paper piercer. We protected the tip of the paper piercer by covering it with a cosmetic sponge.

Think outside the box:
I shopped for containers at Target, ShopKo and office supply stores. I've also found great containers at hardware, sporting goods, grocery, kitchen and bath stores. Make sure the containers fit your needs—that you're not fitting your needs to the containers.

Note: We assembled Gail's shelves inside the closet since that's the only way they would fit. To make use of the other side of the closet, we stacked small

Sterilite drawers to fill the space where the upper hanging area had been. We used a larger set of Sterilite drawers on the bottom. The drawers are especially handy in that they can be pulled out easily and taken to your workspace, then returned when you're finished.

Label everything: We labeled each drawer. In the larger drawers, we labeled items within the drawer and used smaller organizers to further divide the space.

Wrapping Up

When we were through (see photo above), Gail was pleased. She knew where all her supplies were, and she had a place to put them after using them.

When you're through organizing your own space, take time to evaluate. Have you met your goals? As you get new supplies, purge old supplies you won't use and integrate the new supplies into your system. Don't be afraid to try new configurations. This is your space—adjust it to meet your needs.

You may think some people are born organized. Not true! Organization is a skill that can be learned. Apply these principles, give yourself time to work through each step, and you will find the organizational side of scrapbooking so much simpler. I know you can do it!

Read on for Gail's input and an itemized look at costs.

Welcome to scrapbook supply heaven! Everything has a place and is easy to access in seconds.

TIP: Expanding file pockets (regular or hanging styles) are ideal for organizing memorabilia.

TIP: Many containers designed for scrapbookers are meant for "on the go" use more than "home" use. Always consider ease of retrieval and putting things away.

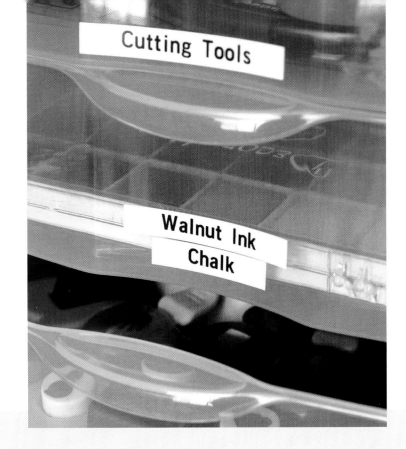

Cutting Tools

Walnut Ink
Chalk

Put a colored sheet of cardstock in a page protector (left). Place solid-colored paper scraps in front of the cardstock and patterned-paper scraps in back. Store the scraps in an acrylic container.

Label everything (right). Subdivide drawers as needed. Keep items attached to the cardboard they came on, or place them in small plastic bags.

my closet makeover by Gail Robinson

I consider myself organized, and people who know me would probably agree.

On the other hand, my husband would call me obsessive. What can I say? I like things neat. Still, when it comes to my scrapbooking stuff . . .

The trouble began with my cart. When I bought it, I had room for everything. As I purchased more items than my cart could hold, my supplies became chaos. *Creating Keepsakes* asked if I would be willing to have a closet reorganized so it would hold all of my supplies. My answer? Of course!

Patti Coombs was the talented organizer sent to help, and she is awesome! As a scrapbooker, she knew exactly what questions to ask. After some discussion, we pinned down my goals. I wanted:

- a space to store my paper so it's more accessible

- a better way to store my fibers (Patti says that, aside from Lisa Bearnson, I have the largest fiber collection she's ever seen)

- a system to store my scraps (I am definitely a saver)

I knew that when we were through I would be organized, but I had no idea how detailed Patti would be. Everything has a place, and I mean everything! You can see several solutions in the photos shown with this article. More ideas?

- Patti turned wire crates on their sides and tied dividers in them for my paper (see photo on page 22). We chose the crates because they offered the best use of space. The dividers are attached with plastic wire ties (often available by the electrical tape in hardware stores).

- Patti put a piece of cardboard in a page protector and placed it on the bottom of each "shelf." This makes it easier to slide paper in and out of the crates.

While I may make small changes here and there, I love what Patti's done. I feel so much more organized. Now, if only I can keep it that way! →

organize

what patti supplied and what it cost

Here's a quick list of what it took to organize Gail's closet.

Store	Supplies	Cost
Target	One set of wire crates	19.99
	Three-drawer wide drawers	16.99
	Wire shelf units	39.98 (two at 19.99)
Office Depot	Label tape	13.67
	Pencil box	.25
ShopKo	Small three-drawer organizers (six at 3.99)	23.94
	Plastic shoe box	1.37
	Kitchen utensil box	5.00
	Drawer organizer baskets (three at 1.00)	3.00
Roberts	12" x 12" page protectors	6.99
	Acrylic box	.99
OfficeMax	Legal-size desktop file	12.99
	Tech file (two at 4.99)	9.98
	Memorabilia file (two at 5.99)	11.98
	Legal-size desktop file	12.99
	Legal-size folders	9.29
Total:		**$189.40**

TIP: Use plastic wire ties to attach extra shelves and keep them steady.

TIP: When planning, consider if you're right- or left-handed and position items accordingly. Make your space work for you. ♥

organization tips from readers

The editors at CK love how resourceful our readers are. Keep coming up with handy solutions, and don't forget about the great organizational products already on the market.

Tackle That Mess

While shopping with my husband at a hardware store, I found a great organizational tool: tackle boxes! They include compartments for almost everything, and some boxes even have wheels.

My favorite tackle box is the Bucket Buddy, which comes in large and small sizes. I use the outside compartments for my scissors, my pens and other tools, while the inside of the bucket is perfect for holding trash while I work.

—*Renee Erzinger*
Palm Bay, FL

Photo Organizer

My photos always seemed unorganized until I purchased a large, under-the-bed plastic box with a lid. The box holds two rows of film and easily accommodates 60 envelopes of double prints.

Each time I get a roll of film developed, I write the date and event on the envelope. The envelope is filed into my box in chronological order. When I complete my scrapbooking for an event, I write "Done" on the envelope and file it. The box is divided into several categories: completed events, seasons and years. Now I can keep track of where I left off!

—*Mary Miller, Ballwin, MO*

Tips & Tricks

On-the-Go Cropper

When I go to local crops, I usually don't need a lot of supplies but I do need mobility. To make my Crop-in-Style Jr. easier to transport, I mounted wheels to the case.

First I placed a clear piece of 1/4"-thick plexiglass on the outside bottom of the case. I then placed a second piece underneath the foam panel on the inside bottom. I drilled a hole through each corner and mounted casters. Now I have a Crop-in-Style Jr. on wheels!

—Judith Bauer, Archer, FL

Scrap Solutions

I keep a small galvanized bucket on my desk to hold paper scraps while I scrapbook. When it's full, I sort the scraps by color. If the pieces are big enough, I punch them. If not, I get out the blender and make handmade paper.

—Shannon Gleaves, Hobbs, NM

Ink Storage Containers

When I first set up my stamping and scrapbooking room, I needed an inexpensive way to organize my inkpads. After discovering that each inkpad is approximately the size of a cassette tape, I found the perfect solution: a wall-mounted cassette storage case. It lets me store the ink pads upside-down, which is ideal!

—Joellyn Clark, Sandy, UT

Spice Rack Solution

My neighbor was getting rid of a revolving spice rack and asked if I wanted it. With 12 jars, it's perfect for small embellishments such as eyelets, charms, extra punches and other little trinkets. I label each jar using my Xyron machine. The rack looks great on my desk, and everything is accessible with the turn of my hand!

—Kristi Russell, Valdosta, GA

Template Organizer

When I store templates in a three-ring binder, I trace an outline of each template onto white or light-colored paper. The templates and paper are stored together in sheet protectors. That way, when I use a particular template, I know exactly where to put it away.

This also helps when my children "borrow" my templates. I can tell which ones haven't been returned, and the outlines help my children know where to put the templates when they finish using them. This organizer is also a big help at crops.

—Sherry Jackson, Bristol, TN

Hanging Jars

To organize small embellishments such as eyelets and punched shapes, mount plastic jars to the bottom of a shelf. (Baby food jars or eight-ounce peanut-butter jars work great.) Drill a hole in the top of the lid, then drill a pilot hole underneath the shelf. Affix the lid to the shelf with a wood screw.

The lids stay in place and hold the jars in the empty space under the shelf. To retrieve the jar's contents, just unscrew the jar from the lid and screw the jar back when you're done. This utilizes unused space with minimal cost.

—Jackye Bowen, Covington, GA

Memorabilia Sorter

Nothing is worse than creating the perfect page, then discovering you have no room for your carefully saved memorabilia. Here's how I avoid that frustration:

I purchase a twelve-month, accordion-style pocket folder for each year. As I collect memorabilia from events (school programs, ticket stubs, cards and more), I place them in chronological order in the monthly pockets. (I put the latest item at the back of the appropriate pocket.)

When I'm ready to scrapbook an event, even months later, I simply check the memorabilia pocket that corresponds to the date of the pictures.

—Kristy Lee, Bad Aibling, Germany

OVER-THE-DOOR PHOTO HANGER

To organize pictures so they're easily visible and always at my fingertips, I purchased an over-the-door plastic shoe holder. With its 24 clear pockets, I can group my photos according to the layout, then insert them into the pockets, which fit up to 4" x 6" photos.

When I'm ready, I quickly grab a group of pictures. I jot down a few ideas on Post-It notes, then stick them on the outside of the related pocket. The best part is that my room is now decorated with colorful photos of friends, family and vacations. It's a great source of inspiration as I work on my scrapbook!

—Melissa Draper, Orem, UT

Creating K

preparing *for a* CROP

Maximize your crop time by getting organized

by Becky Higgins

It's six-thirty. You've fed your family, and you're in a mad rush to gather your scrapbooking supplies before your seven o'clock crop. You wonder which pictures to scrap, which supplies you need, and if you should bother taking your entire album. Most of all, you wonder, "Why, oh *why*, didn't I think about all of this earlier?"

Imagine being able to waltz out the door, completely organized and ready to tackle several layouts. Imagine not having to transport boatloads of product to and from your car, but making it in (gasp) just *one* trip! Imagine your cropping friends' admiration when they see you actually completing several layouts instead of sifting through a dozen envelopes of recently developed pictures. Here are some ideas to help you make the most of your precious crop time.

Figures 1–4. Create a series of layouts using the same basic supplies. *Pages by Becky Higgins.* **Supplies** *Patterned paper:* SEI; *Tags:* Making Memories; *Alphabet stamps:* PSX Design; *Stamping ink:* ColorBox, Clearsnap; *Computer font:* CK Primary, "The Art of Creative Lettering" CD, *Creating Keepsakes.*

on your mark, get set ...

Ask yourself, "What do I want to accomplish at this crop?" Remember that this is a social gathering. If you're going for just a few hours and plan to catch up with your friends or admire other people's albums, you'll be lucky to finish a page or two.

On the other hand, if you're attending an all-day scrap-a-thon, you're probably anxious to get down to business. Depending on your preparation and how fast you scrapbook, you can even set a goal to complete a dozen layouts.

Regardless of your time allotment, be realistic. Do as much pre-crop planning as you can so you won't waste crop time.

PRODUCTS *on the* GO

Leaving the kitchen table behind and cropping on the go? The following products can help keep you organized!

Organizing Photos, Papers, Pages and Accents

Next time you need to organize your photos, papers, pages and embellishments, consider sheet protectors (one page per sheet protector) or an accordion-style organizer (one layout per section). Here are great finds that can help. Check your local scrapbook supply store. *Note:* Be sure to also check the company web sites. Most include more information on organizational and storage solutions.

Caren's Crafts (*www.scrapbooking4fun.com*)
• Scrap-N-File Expanding Organizer, $15.95
• Scrap-N-File Tote, $18
• Scrap-N-File Photomate, $29.99
• Scrap-N-File Companion files, $4.99 (lightweight 3-pack) and $5.99 (heavyweight 3-pack)

PLan YOUR PaGeS

The key to crop success can be summed up in one word—preparation. You can do that by finding your focus. Envision your end result. Perhaps you'll work on completing a theme or gift album. Pull together any papers and embellishments you think you'll need.

For example, at a recent crop I knew I wanted to finish the layouts for my family's Disney cruise album. I wanted the layouts to have a similar feel, so I chose coordinating papers, cardstock and tags for my titles (see Figures 1–4). I imagined my layouts as fresh, simple in design, and—most importantly—*completed* by the end of the evening. I achieved my goal because I planned ahead and envisioned the completed pages.

Crop-in-Style *(www.cropinstyle.com)*

Photo Holder, $14.95

PT Portfolio, $19.95

Paper Taker, $24.95 (8½" x 11") and $29.95 (12" x 12")

Cropper Hopper by Leeco Industries *(www.cropperhopper.com)*

Paper Protector, $5.25 (8½" x 11") and $5.95 (12" x 12")

Expandable Paper Organizer, $11.95

This day was my personal favorite. Disney's private island, Castaway Cay, is, in my opinion, the perfect beach. The sand was white, the water clear (and no giant waves, which I don't particularly care for). It was also a gorgeous day and only started to rain just as we were boarding the ship at the end of the day. They had great places to eat, some fun souvenir shops, water sports and more. As a family, we parked ourselves at a great location and stayed there most of the day. We played volleyball and enjoyed watching the cousins splash around together in the ocean.

KNOWING IS HALF THE BATTLE

Scrapbook pages involve two types of tasks: mind-oriented and hand-oriented. Determining how to position your pictures or figuring out what to include in your journaling are tasks that use your mind. Setting eyelets, cutting out template letters and chalking die cuts require handwork but not a lot of brain power.

Try to do your "mind" tasks *before* the crop. When you think of layout ideas, sketch them! (See Figure 5.) Keep design notes with the pictures and papers you plan to use for each layout. Trust me—when you're ready to create the pages, your job will be easier. "Hands-on" tasks like matting photos and punching are perfect activities while you chat with your neighbors.

The bottom line? Know what you can handle during distracting times and what needs to be thought out before the crop.

Generations
(www.generationsnow.com)

Memory Express, with the K & Company designer look, $19.99

Photo Express, with the K & Company designer look, $14.99

Weekender Backpack, $35.99

Sassy Scrapper, $7.99

Scrapfolio, $14.99

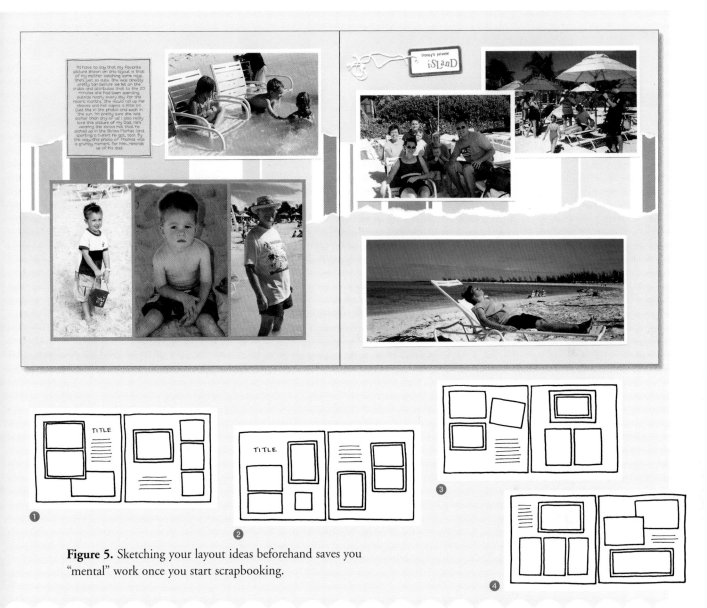

Figure 5. Sketching your layout ideas beforehand saves you "mental" work once you start scrapbooking.

Mochalatte (*www.mochalatte.com*)

Super Tote Box, $11.95

Scrapping & Accessories Organizer, $18.75
(12" x 12") and $10.35 (sized for photos)

Scrapbook Sally (*www.scrapbooksally.com*)

Paper Packer, $29.95

Organizing the Rest of Your Stuff

Of course you'll need a place for everything *else*, including basic supplies, tools and miscellaneous necessities (such as that bag of peanut M&Ms to share and CDs to listen to). You can find everything from small carrying cases to large wheeled totes. Check your local scrapbook supply store. You can also check each company's web site. Most include more information on organizational and storage solutions.

Kokuyo (877/465-6589)

Kaddy supply tote, $9.99

Cropper Hopper by Leeco Industries
(www.cropperhopper.com)

- Scrapbook Tote Bag, $34.95
- Flat Pack, $17.95
- All Terrain Bag, $129.95
- Supply cases, $12.95–27.95
- Embellishment Organizer, $12.95

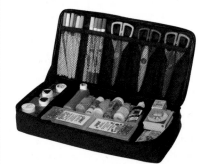

Plaid (www.plaidenterprises.com)

Creative Gear Craft Tote, $54.99

Generations
(www.generationsnow.com)

Crop 'n Carry Scrapbooking Tote, $42.99

Denim Crop Caddy, $129.99

Crop Station, $129.99

Create-a-Bag Crop Station, $85.99

Memory Tote, $74.99

gather your supplies

Now that you've grouped your photos, papers and embellishments, you need to gather everything else. What are the basic supplies you use every time you scrapbook? For me, it's my paper trimmer, a small pair of scissors, a journaling pen, ruler, eraser, pencil and adhesive tabs. Make sure you take any additional tools that could come in handy for these specific layouts, such as chalk, templates, punches or eyelet-setting tools.

Decide which items aren't necessary. Ask a friend if she will share her colored pencils. Offer to share your paper trimmer. Sharing saves you space and hassle. As tempting as it is to haul all of your new gadgets, a bin filled with fiber and your latest 13 rolls of film, it's just not practical if you're serious about completing several pages. It's distracting and you'll lose focus.

Scrapbook Sally
(www.scrapbooksally.com)

Tote Bag, $49.95

Crop-in-Style
(www.cropinstyle.com)

Various totes, $39.95–129.95

Tool bag, $24.95

Back Pack, $39.95

Stamp, Scrap n' Roll *(www.stampscrapnroll.com)*

Mini Duffel, $12.99

The ScrapRack
(www.thescraprack.com)

TravelPack, $28.95

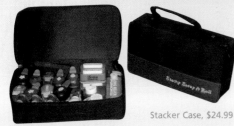

Stacker Case, $24.99

Tutto
(www.tutto.com)

Crafts On Wheels bag, $139.99

SIMPLIFY THE PROCESS

When I'm in the comfort of my home and every product I own is within reach, there's no telling what I'll work on.

At a crop, the environment is social and I'll likely get sidetracked. Focus on completing layouts with the same theme, such as the Disney cruise album I mentioned earlier. If you're chatting with friends and looking at their work, simplifying your own work could mean accomplishing your crop goals.

save THE BEST FOR LAST

Here's my most helpful tip: Save the journaling for when you get home. If you're like me, it's hard to concentrate on meaningful journaling when you're being distracted by conversations. Create your journaling block, even draw your pencil guidelines, then finish the writing part later. Or, if you prefer computer journaling, be sure to leave enough space for it.

Your expressions, feelings, memories and thoughts are just as important as the pictures. Reserve the "mind-ful" task of writing for when you can really dedicate your genuine thoughts to what you want to say. When I try to write journaling with lots of people and noise around, it ends up as meaningless chatter that states the obvious and doesn't say what I really want to express. ♥

ArtBin (www.artbin.com)

Mega Tote, $49.95

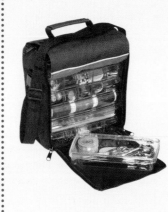

Quick Tote, $27.95

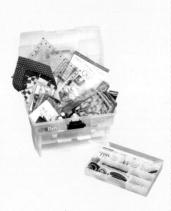

Storganizer, $44.95

Tote Express, $145

Double Take, $18.95

Sidekick, $14.99

Tote 'N Go, $52.99

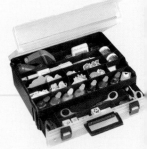

The Top Drawer, $29.99

Journaling Checklist

Ask yourself these questions when journaling on your next layout:

☐ Did I go beyond obvious statements like "We had a great time"? Did I include meaningful details that will make the memory more vivid?

☐ Did I supply the who, what, when, where and why for historical value?

☐ Did I write my journaling from the perspective of what I think people years—even generations—from now will want to know?

☐ Did I eliminate details that could embarrass me or someone else?

☐ Did I include the perspective of family and friends if applicable?

☐ Did I provide more insight on the page subject's personality?

Title Placement

Tired of always placing a title at the top of a scrapbook page? Try something different! Here are four fresh ideas from Becky Higgins for title placement:

❶ Include your title on the same block or strip with your journaling and a photo.

❷ Put each letter of your title on a strip and alternate heights.

❸ Make the title an integral part of a photo collage.

❹ Place a strip of cardstock across your page and use your title as a border between photos

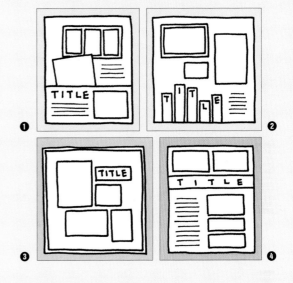

Creative Framing

To add visual interest to a picture, "frame" your subject with items like:

◆ A curving tree branch
◆ Colorful balls or objects (see example)
◆ A doorway or arched hallway
◆ A window frame or picture frame
◆ Your subject looking through an object

Fast Storage for Fibers and Floss

Want a clever way to store thread, fibers and floss? Use plastic bobbins, says Allison Strine of Atlanta, Georgia. Allison wraps fiber and other materials around plastic bobbins, then hooks them on a large ring (similar to a key chain). The packages of 28 plastic bobbins and a metal ring can be found at most craft and notions stores.

30 School Solutions

tackle those pictures and projects today

Six months ago, my husband asked me the same question he's asked the past six years: "Will you ever get our kids' school stuff out of boxes and folders and into albums?" I cringed, because despite my best intentions, I'm way behind. Can you relate? If so, breathe a little easier—help is on the way! You'll find 30 fresh solutions on the pages that follow.

by jana lillie

Create a Mini-Album

Showcase school pictures in an easy-to-maintain format

BY MARY LARSON

Education is not received. It is achieved.
Author Unknown

SCHOOL YEARS
Wyatt
2000
2001
2002

First Grade

Second Grade

Third Grade

Fourth Grade

Ever since I was in grade school, I've seen those 13-slotted frames where you can put a school picture every year. Great idea! When my sons started school, I wanted to do something similar, but more flexible.

I decided to create a 6" x 6" mini-album to showcase school photos and keep track of my sons' changing looks. After designing a school-themed cover, I included a library card and pocket inside to keep track of the school years.

I made the inside pages very simple, with just a place for photos and the grade. The pages are large enough to add a child's signature, teacher information and more. Because I started the project after my oldest son had started school, I couldn't have him sign each page. I plan to go through my son's school papers from previous years to find the signatures I need.

At the back of the book, I included a place for the list of schools attended. *Note:* Leave enough lines for elementary, junior and high schools, plus extras spaces if you think your family could move or your child might change schools.

These books are easy to make and keep up with. Best of all, when they're completed your child will have a wonderful keepsake!

Just the other day, my daughter ran over and exclaimed, "Mommy, I can't believe you threw my school paper in the garbage!" She pulled a worksheet out of the garbage can to show me the row of lowercase a's she'd painstakingly written. We put the paper into a tall pile of her favorite schoolwork, and I thought, "What am I going to do with all these papers?"

My daughter is in preschool, yet my calculations are that she'll bring home over a thousand papers this year. As a scrapbooking mom, I need a method to decide what to scrapbook, what to shred, and what to store. Here's a plan for how to manage and preserve your child's school memories for future generations.

DON'T PILE IT—FILE IT

1 Choose a filing system so you can safely tuck papers away until you're ready to sort through them. You might like a color-coded, hanging file folder system or a literature sorter from an office supply store.

Choose themes for each category, such as "daily assignments," "artwork," "practice papers" and "tests." Your child can help file papers each night when she comes home from school.

2 Go through your file folders once a month. Decide what's important to save and what can be tossed. I suggest saving the following: self-portraits, first efforts, essays or short stories that give insight into your child's personality, tests or reports with exceptional scores, and your child's best or favorite pieces of artwork. In addition, save projects that have a special story attached to them (I still have an old math test that I struggled to pass! It's not my best score ever, but it shows the value of not giving up.)

SAFE STORAGE SOLUTIONS

Ready to take the next step? Here are several solutions for preserving your child's treasured school memories:

1 Scan favorite pages and print them with archivally safe ink on acid-free paper. (*Tip:* You can scan the images full size, then reduce file sizes so you can fit 2–4 pages per sheet of paper. This will save paper and storage space.) Slip pages into sheet protectors and store in binders clearly labeled with each school year. You now have archival copies that won't crumble or fade over time!

2 Snap a photograph of your child with his or her favorite artwork once a month. At the end of the year, create an "Artwork Throughout the Year" scrapbook page. (You'll enjoy seeing how your child's artwork changes and he or she has grown throughout the year!)

An alternative? Store pictures in acid-free photo albums.

3 Store original copies and scanned images in memory storage boxes. I like the Document Boxes ($8–$10) from Archival Methods (*www.archivalmethods.com*) and the Museum Storage Boxes ($11–$28) from Dick Blick (*www.dickblick.com*).

4 Don't want to deal with paper copies? Scan and save schoolwork and digital photographs to CDs for an easy storage solution.

Scrapbook Your Child's School Portrait

Experiment with these 10 fresh approaches

Figure 1. Give school photos a more "grown-up" look with artistic touches like embossing and gold edging. *Page by Heather Uppencamp.* **Supplies** *Patterned paper:* Colors By Design; *Embossing powder:* Stampendous!; *Brass:* Paragona, Art Emboss; *Stamping ink:* ColorBox, Clearsnap.

You could scrapbook your child's picture as is, but why not have a little artistic fun if your creative spirit beckons? Consider the following approaches:

❶ Go holographic. Make your child a star by including his or her picture on a holographic background that's sure to dazzle.

❷ Include your child's inked handprint or a hand mold (made from handmade paper) alongside the picture.

❸ Have your child draw a self-portrait and include it with his or her school portrait.

❹ Add dramatic flourish with artistic embossing and stamping. Heather Uppencamp dressed up her daughter's portrait page (see Figure 1) with stamped-looking background paper, embossed leaf accents, and decorative gold edging around the portrait.

To create a decorative gold edge like that in the "Rachel" page, carefully tear the portrait's edges. Cut a piece of cardstock ¼" smaller on all sides than the picture. Hold the cardstock over the portrait, apply stamping ink to the exposed portion of the picture, then heat-emboss the ink with embossing powder.

Figure 2. Make your child the star attraction by "framing" his or her school picture. *Page by Nichol Magouirk.* **Supplies** *Vellum, photo accent and letter stickers:* Creative Imaginations; *Metal-rimmed tag, date eyelet and metal letters:* Making Memories; *Silver letter stickers:* Stampendous!; *Small tags:* American Tag Company; *Dotlets:* Doodlebug Design; *Stamping ink (to "age" frame):* Hero Arts; *Other:* Thread and nailheads.

MAKING MEMORIES

SCRAPWORKS

MY MIND'S EYE

Figure 3. Add flair to your child's photo with a slide holder or metal or paper frame.

5 Use a "frame" approach. Center your child's picture on a page, then "frame" it with blocks that contain school and year, favorite friends, teacher (and note, if available), the year's big events and more. Continue to a facing page if desired. You can also include handwriting samples, reduced images of artwork and more.

6 Embellish the area around the picture with decorative punch or die-cut designs.

7 Keep the focus on your child with a simple yet sophisticated page design. For the third-grade picture of her son Chad, note how Nichol Magouirk spotlighted his picture by framing it against solid colors of cardstock (Figure 2). Her apple, staple and letter accents help convey a sense of "school."

8 "Frame" small school pictures with slide holders. Or, use metal or paper frames. (See Figure 3.)

9 Include a note from you and a note from the teacher.

10 Create an interactive "schoolhouse" layout, complete with windows that open to show your child's class portraits through the years.

A Teacher's Request

Help capture the school experience

BY DARCEE THOMPSON

When a student from eight years ago came to visit me the other day, she could only recall one thing from my class. I had to hide my disappointment, because we'd done a lot of fun things that year. I wished I'd done a better job helping her document her year in first grade. Since then, I've committed to making a bigger difference as a mom and as a teacher.

Each year, my students and I experience several fun events (Gingerbread Day, Space Camp, Bubble Day and more) that are worth recording. I carry a camera so I can take pictures, but all too often I get distracted by the need to direct traffic, manage students or take care of loose ends. What I could really use is a parent to help document these fun days.

GET INVOLVED

How can you as a parent and scrapbooker help? Volunteer to assist the teacher on field trips. Bring your camera (I would love more photo options for year-end books or movies). If you show up often, students will get used to you and your camera quickly, and you'll get more real-life pictures.

Aside from the "big events," be aware of the everyday events that are picture-worthy. Ask the teacher's permission, then bring your camera and see if you can sneak in candid pictures of the following:

✓ A child immersed in a book

✓ A child with his or her teacher

✓ A child working on an art project

✓ A child playing outdoors at recess

✓ A child with his or her best friends

✓ A child showing off his or her cubicle or desk

✓ A child walking to school or waiting for the bus

✓ A child in front of the school, its name on a sign in the background

Need more ideas? Think of what you wish you remembered about grade school. Partway into the school year, ask what your child would like to have documented about his or her grade, teacher and classroom. Make an effort to get those pictures.

School is such a big part of a child's life. Do what you can to help him or her remember the high points and everyday events for years to come!

Create a layout that showcases your child's teacher, friends, cubicle and more. *Pages by Noralee Peterson.* **Supplies** *Patterned paper:* Provo Craft; *Die cuts and frame:* O'Scrap!, Imaginations; *Eyelets:* Doodlebug Design; *Pen:* Zig Twin Tip, EK Success.

CHALK IT. Chalk's not just for blackboards! With the new Chalklets by EK Success (*www.eksuccess.com*), you can add primary or pastel colors to your school pages. The chalks are sold individually in eight-color palettes (Toy Box, Nursery Rhymes or Surprise), or choose the 24-color value pack.

Page by Wendy Sue Anderson. **Supplies** *Chalk:* Chalklets, EK Success; *Letter stickers (chalked over, then removed for title):* Liz King, EK Success; *Letter stickers for date:* SEI; *Eyelets:* Doodlebug Design (red) and Making Memories (apple); *Computer font:* CK Constitution, "Fresh Fonts" CD, *Creating Keepsakes; Other:* Slide holder and ribbon.

PUNCH IT. School's all about letters, and so is the QuickKutz die-cut system (*www.quickutz.com*). Punch out the shapes you need—it's ABC easy—then embellish them if desired.

Page by Julie Scattaregia. **Supplies** *"Heart" die-cut letters:* QuicKutz; *Papers:* Kangaroo & Joey (patterned) and Stamp It Up (solid); *Vellum:* The Paper Company; *Computer font:* CK Journaling, "The Best of Creative Lettering" CD Combo, *Creating Keepsakes; Punches:* EK Success (small flower), Emagination Crafts (heart) and Family Treasures (daisy); *Letter stickers, poemstones, faux wax seal, stickers, brad and letter rub-ons:* Creative Imaginations; *Embossing enamel:* UTEE, Suze Weinberg; *Vellum tag and brads:* Making Memories; *Fibers:* EK Success; *Other:* Transparency. *Idea to note:* Julie inked her die-cut letters with embossing ink, applied embossing enamel, then heated it. Whenever you want to emboss an image and can't find the right stamp, look to your punches, letter or shape templates.

Pages by Kristi Barnes. **Supplies** *Rubber stamps, embossing powder and chalk:* Stampin' Up!; *Stamping ink:* VersaMark, Tsukineko; *Square punch:* Family Treasures; *Computer font:* CK Handprint, "The Best of Creative Lettering" CD Combo, *Creating Keepsakes.*

STAMP IT. Want to create simple yet stylish accents for your school pages? Stamp and emboss them! Stampin' Up! (*www.stampinup.com*) offers a variety of playful images to accent but not overwhelm your school pictures.

MAT IT. Mat school pictures, notes, school logos and more in style with custom mats by School Memory Corp. (*www.schoolmemory.com*). Made from 4-ply Crescent mat board, the 11¾" x 11¾" photo mats fit comfortably in top-loading, 12" x 12" page protectors and scrapbooks. Visit the company's web site for pricing and a variety of format options. Turn your scrapbook page into an elegant "picture frame."

Write On!

through Kindergarten

LINE IT UP. Learning to write is a big first step in a child's life. Showcase early attempts on attractive lined paper like that from MiniGraphics (*www.minigraphics.com*).

Pages by Wendy Sue Anderson. **Supplies** *Patterned paper:* MiniGraphics; *Letter stickers:* me & my BIG ideas; *Flower eyelet accents:* Classy Accents; *Thread:* Scrapbook Stitches, Making Memories; *Computer font:* CK Constitution, "Fresh Fonts" CD, *Creating Keepsakes.*

Write On!

through Kindergarten

I see
I see You
I
Meagan BOOKS

Since you were a toddler you've had an obsession with books. You preferred books over most of your toys. As soon as you could grip a pencil, you were "writing." When you started to realize that the funny little shapes on the pages were letters, and that when they were put together in a certain way they created words, you wanted to learn how to make them. Now you are in kindergarten and you know how to make each letter, the sound it makes, and how to put letters together to form words. You love to sit and write, practicing each letter over & over. You are a great writer – even your teacher says you are! May '03

SHAKE IT UP. Add plastic letters (available at craft and general-interest stores), beads and more to a shaker box. The letters add a playful yet academic touch. Get ready to rattle and roll!

Page by Kristy Banks. **Supplies** *Tiny buttons:* Buttons Galore; *Plastic letters:* From Wal-Mart; *Computer font:* CK Constitution, "Fresh Fonts" CD, *Creating Keepsakes;* *Other:* Ribbon.

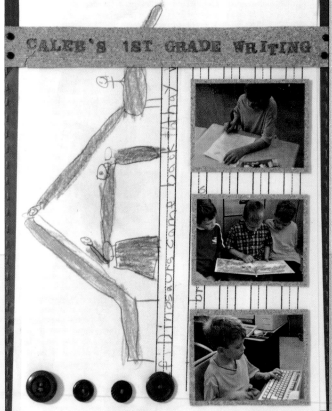

POCKET IT. Transparencies aren't just for overhead projectors—use the acid-free variety to create page pockets that hold school memorabilia! Here, Darcee Thompson cut a transparency down to 8½" x 10½", then stitched it to a piece of cardstock.

After stamping her cork with heated metal stamps, Darcee trimmed the student work down to 7¾" x 10½" so it would fit in the pocket. She then adhered photos and buttons to the top of the transparency.

Page by Darcee Thompson. **Supplies** *Transparency:* Pockets on a Roll, F&M Enterprises; *Cork and buttons:* Magic Scraps; *Embroidery thread:* JP Coats; *Other:* Brads.

Windows, wheelies, sliders and pop-ups—these terms sound like they'd be more at home on a baseball diamond or at a dirt-bike race than on a scrapbook page. Actually, these items are interactive elements that can help you showcase multiple photos on one page. A few of the benefits for school pages?

> You can easily see how your children have changed through the years.

> When you scrapbook your children's photos, you build self-esteem. Kids love to look at "their" pages over and over again and know that you wanted to document their lives.

> Making school pages interactive makes them more fun. Children (and adults!) love to spin, pull or open an interactive item to reveal the hidden faces of self or friends.

Following are examples of windows, wheelies, sliders and pop-ups. Give them a try! You can find patterns online at *www.creatingkeepsakes.com/magazine*.

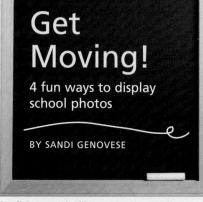

Get Moving!

4 fun ways to display school photos

BY SANDI GENOVESE

Sandi Genovese is Ellison senior vice president and creative director.

windows closed

3 windows opened

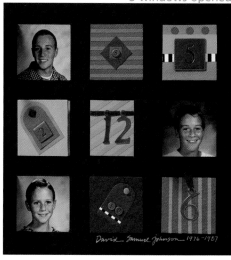

Supplies *Window die cut:* Ellison; *Tag dies:* Sizzix; *Paper:* Canson; *Metal numbers:* Making Memories; *Colored bradlets:* Provo Craft; *Hole punches:* Fiskars; *Silver pen:* Pigma Micron, Sakura; *Glue dots:* Glue Dots International; *Adhesives:* Xyron and double-stick tape.

WINDOWS

Open each window, and you'll see that the boy's shirts in his school portraits were usually geometric prints. I continued that theme by decorating the windows with geometric patterns like stripes, checks and dots. Each grade is indicated with a metal number that sits over the geometric design. I used glue dots to fasten the metal numbers to the windows.

Next, die cut the top sheet (or use the Ellison pattern supplied online) and fold on the creases to create the windows. Place the photos on an 8" x 8" backing sheet so they'll show through the windows. (I cut a second window sheet from copy paper and cut out each window to use as a template for perfect positioning of the photos.) The window sheet is attached to the back sheet with adhesive around the edges and in the channels between the windows.

Top: Front of closed slider card. *Middle:* Slider card opened. *Bottom:* Open slider card with pulled portion revealing Sandi's picture today.

SLIDERS

When I found my old school photos from fourth to eighth grade, I decided to incorporate them into a more vintage look to complement the black-and-white photos. The slider card has a front cover and two surfaces inside to decorate, as well as a fourth area that's exposed when the slider portion is pulled.

I chose black, cream and rust colors (along with scrabble letter tiles and a chrome drawer label) to enhance the vintage look. It's always easier to journal on lined paper, so I drew lines to replicate the look of elementary school paper for my journaling.

Supplies *Slider die:* Ellison; *Tag dies:* Sizzix; *Paper:* Canson; *Silver drawer label:* Magic Scraps; *Black and silver pens:* Pigma Micron, Sakura; *Red bradlet:* Provo Craft; *Chalk:* Craf-T Products; *Other:* Scrabble letter tiles.

outside

Supplies *Wheel dies:* Ellison; *Patterned paper:* NRN Designs; *Paper:* Canson; *Heart brad:* Provo Craft; *Letter and number stickers:* Making Memories; *Checkered stickers:* Mrs. Grossman's; *Pop dots:* All Night Media; *Adhesive:* Xyron.

inside

inside

WHEELIES

A photo wheel is the perfect place to feature the smallest school-size photos. Die-cut flashcard wheels provide the format for 10 separate photos.

I cut the girl's photo wheel from zebra and bright-colored paper to reflect her love of animals and vivid color. The openings in the front wheel dictate the placement of photos and grade level on the back wheel. The two wheels are held together with a heart-shaped brad, making it easy to turn the wheel to the next photo. Note how I adapted the same concept to pictures of a boy and nine of his friends from a class photo.

outside

Supplies *Pop-up die:* Ellison; *Patterned paper:* Anna Griffin; *Heart charm:* Making Memories; *Pen:* Zig Writer, EK Success; *Adhesives:* Xyron and double-stick tape.

POP-UPS

The motion of opening and closing a pop-up card helps pictures "come to life." This pop-up card has five tabs for photo placement. Simply die-cut the card in your scrapbook store (or use the pattern provided online) and fold on the creases. A slightly larger card cover encases the pop-up card.

Follow a Formula

Identify the repeat elements

Does the thought of coming up with a fresh scrapbooking approach for each school year scare you? Worry no more! Identify the repeat elements you want to scrapbook for each school year (such as student portrait, class photo, favorite memories and more), then create a spread that presents those elements in an effective way. Each year, simply "plug" updated elements into the same basic page design, adding a few custom touches if desired. ❤

The Perfection Trap

Are you stuck in it?

Guess why I got this article assignment? Yep, I'm a perfectionist.
I'm guilty of all the perfectionist traits: I'm the only one who sees a mistake on my layout. I'm afraid to try new techniques because, well, what if I fail? I'll redo a layout over and over again to get it *just* right.

So, what's a perfectionist to do? Instead of starting a scrapbook therapy group, I went to five scrapbookers I admire and trust and asked for their advice. If you get stuck in the perfection trap, you may find their advice helpful—heaven knows I did!

by Tracy White   Illustration by Betsy Everitt

Julie Turner's Advice

Julie avoids the perfection trap by keeping perspective. Here's how she does it:

1. A perfect page is not my highest priority. When I pursue perfection on a layout, I often lose sight of the lives and relationships I'm scrapbooking. Yes, I love the creative process, but I need to keep it in perspective. For example, I'll ask myself, "Will anyone notice a small detail that doesn't seem quite right to me? Does it affect the message I'm communicating on the layout?" If not, I leave the layout alone and move on—even if I'm not perfectly satisfied.

2. Photographs are the most important element. If I start with strong photos, I'm more likely to be pleased with the end result. Good pictures will command attention on an average page, but a dynamite page won't compensate for poor pictures.

3. When experimenting with new ideas and techniques, I have to be willing to work through problems. Occasionally I must accept "less than stellar" results. When I try the techniques on later pages, I know I'll have the advantage of experience and can improve the results. When struggling through new techniques, I keep a friend's advice in mind: "Take joy in the journey."

"Sand, Sun, Water"
by Julie Turner • Gilbert, AZ

Supplies *Patterned paper, tag, fiber, word sticker, definitions and date stamp:* Making Memories; *Gesso and modeling paste:* Liquitex; *Paper clay:* Creative Paperclay Company; *Embossing powder:* Suze Weinberg; *Watercolor:* Peerless Color Laboratories; *Silk ribbon:* Bucilla; *Embossing ink:* Ranger Industries; *Other:* Glass, transparency film and canvas.

Check This Out

Julie used paper clay to make a framework to hold the pieces of glass. You can do this by following these easy steps:

1. Roll out a piece of paper clay—it's just like rolling out a piecrust! *Note:* Place a piece of waxed paper under the clay to keep it from sticking to the counter.
2. Position the glass pieces over the wet clay—they'll act as your template.
3. Use a craft knife to cut around each glass piece.
4. Take off the glass pieces and remove the excess clay.
5. Insert the glass pieces into their respective openings so the clay maintains its shape while drying overnight.
6. If your perfectionist vein takes hold, use a craft knife to trim any rough spots on the dried paper clay. *Note:* If the glass doesn't fit snuggly, use a little glue along the edges to secure it to the frame.

A Quick Quiz

You might be a perfectionist if you:

☐ Crinkle seven pieces of card-stock to get one that's "just perfect."

☐ Avoid collage because you're afraid it'll look messy and cluttered.

☐ Measure your cardstock four times before you cut it (just in case!).

☐ Put off adhering elements to your layout for three weeks—you never know, you may change your mind!

☐ Measure and pre-poke the holes when stitching on your layout.

☐ Use a ruler when tearing paper. Those lines must be straight!

Display page elements under a piece of glass held securely by a paper-clay frame.

Becky Higgins' Advice

Creative editor Becky Higgins turns out hundreds of quality pages a year. Her advice for avoiding the perfection trap?

1. Don't compare yourself to others. I've heard several scrapbookers say, "Well, it's not like so-and-so would do it, but …" Remember why you're scrapbooking in the first place. Are you doing it to be the best scrapbooker among your circle of friends? Probably not. Most likely you're scrapbooking for wonderful, personally meaningful reasons. Keep this perspective in mind as you work on pages and plan projects.

2. I'm way too behind in my scrapbooks to worry about making all my pages perfect. I save my most creative or time-consuming ideas for extra-special pages. I create many of my "in between" layouts in a snap. Simple. Quick. Done. Then I move on to the next one.

3. Let your style guide you. Don't try to copy another person's style if it's really not your own. As you flip through this magazine, for example, you'll find yourself drawn to particular layouts while you gloss over others. This is because certain elements (color schemes, design, photographs and more) appeal to you for one reason or another. Instead of spending time trying to duplicate someone else's style, create what you want.

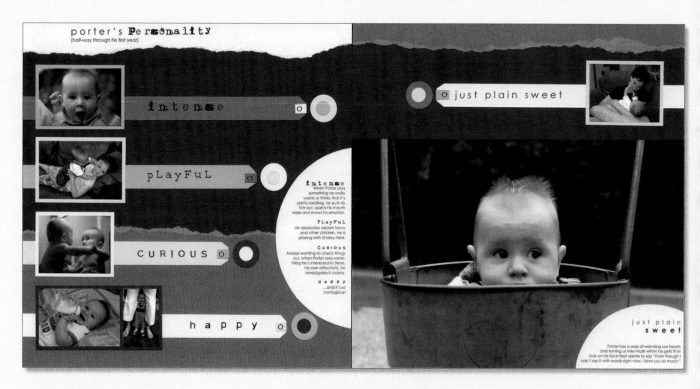

"Porter's Personality"
by Becky Higgins • Cleveland Heights, OH

Supplies *Eyelet stickers:* Stampendous!; *Circle punches:* Family Treasures (large) and EK Success (small); *Computer fonts:* BrentonscrawlType ("Intense") and DeadPostMan ("Happy"), downloaded from *www.free-typewriter-fonts.com*; Keystroke ("Playful"), Becky Higgins' "Creative Clips & Fonts" CD and CK Regal ("Curious"), "Fresh Fonts" CD, *Creating Keepsakes*; Century Gothic ("Just Plain Sweet" and journaling), Microsoft Word.

Rebecca Sower's Advice

CK columnist Rebecca Sower scrapbooks from the heart. She's learned to keep perspective with the following practices:

1. **Picture two quilts side by side.** One is just out of the box from Pottery Barn. The other is a decades-old quilt from Grandma. Sure, the first one may *look* good, perfect and new. But which one *feels* better—not to the touch, but to the heart? Grandma wasn't worried about ruler-straight lines; she just wanted to give something of herself.

2. **For me, striving for the perfect placement and streamlined symmetry takes all the fun out of what I love about scrapbooking—relaxing and letting go!** And remember, most of the time *mistakes are opportunities*!

3. **When's the last time you noticed people taking their rulers out to check up on you as they flipped through the pages of your albums?**

"Baby Rebecca"
by Rebecca Sower
Cedar Hill, TN

Supplies *Script patterned paper:* 7 Gypsies; *Background paper:* Rebecca's own design; *Acrylic paints:* Golden Paints; *Rubber stamps:* John Weber (word), EK Success; Postmodern Design (corner); *Photo corners:* Canson; *Colored pencil:* Prismacolor, Sanford; *Punch:* EK Success; *Embossing powders:* PSX Design and Suze Weinberg; *Gold pen:* Krylon; *Angel:* R.R. Harlee.

Karen Burniston's Advice

Karen Burniston's been in a scrapbooking rut before. Here's how she gets out when she feels "stuck":

1. Trust your gut when in a rut. I used to try every possible color combination and picture placement before committing to a design. Not only did this take "forever," it was mentally exhausting! Now I trust my instincts. Once I find a color scheme, picture placement or accent that works, I use it, even if other great possibilities exist. Now, instead of debating design choices for hours, I'm admiring a finished layout!

2. Fight the blues with tried 'n trues. What's your "comfort technique"? We all have one. Comfort techniques—like paper tearing or stitching—are ones that don't intimidate us because we do them so often. They're the perfect cure for the scrappin' blues. Whenever I feel uninspired and can't find a place to start on a layout, I use a comfort technique to jump-start the process. The technique will often spark a new idea, taking me in a completely different direction.

3. Start with a practice run—I like to call them "warm-up layouts." If I haven't scrapped in a while and I'm feeling uninspired and rusty, I'll choose a set of everyday photos (versus my "showcase photos") and take the pressure off myself to make a fantastic layout.

The idea, of course, is that after finishing the warm-up layout I'll be primed and ready to create a work of art. It's funny how often the warm-up layouts end up being some of my favorites!

"She"
by Karen Burniston
Littleton, CO

Supplies *Patterned papers:* Sonnets, Creative Imaginations; 7 Gypsies; Legacy Collection, Design Originals; *Mesh:* Maruyama, Magenta; *Rub-ons:* Alphawear, Tagwear and Bradwear, Creative Imaginations; *Rubber stamps:* Inkadinkadoo (flower), Rubber Stampede (pattern on heart accent), Rubber Baby Buggy Bumpers (text on lower-left corner), Making Memories (date); *Stamping ink:* StazOn and VersaMark, Tsukineko; ColorBox, Clearsnap; *Embossing powders:* Stampendous! and Suze Weinberg; *Metal-rimmed tags, brad and eyelet:* Making Memories; *Buttons and mesh:* Magic Scraps; *Beads:* JewelCraft; *Letter stickers:* Sonnets, Creative Imaginations; *Ribbon:* Robin's Nest Press; *Metallic pens:* Marvy Uchida; *"Only You" sticker:* Shotz Thoughtz, Creative Imaginations; *Poem:* By Karen Burniston; *Other:* Raffia.

Shannon Wolz's Advice

Through years of teaching, Shannon has realized that many scrapbookers have "rules" or expectations that keep them from having fun. Here's her advice:

1. Do you have your own scrapbooking rules, like "I only do two-page layouts" or "I have to scrapbook every photo"? Get rid of them! Identifying your rules may help you see that many of them limit your creativity. When I recognize my self-imposed rules, I ask myself, "Why?" Then I try to break them.

2. Don't be so concerned with getting caught up that you forget to have fun. I don't even pretend that I'll scrap every picture. Instead, I scrap pictures that I'll have fun scrapbooking or those with a memorable story behind them. Rather than force yourself to scrapbook all your photos (which may set you up to fail), decide what's most important to pass on to your family and start from there.

3. Don't be afraid to make a mistake. I love Marva Collins' quote: "If you can't make a mistake, you can't make anything." When we worry about "messing up," we limit our ability to create. Try new things, take risks, then learn from your experiences and mistakes.

To overcome a fear of making a mistake, try this creativity exercise: Make a scrapbook page as quickly as you can. Use whatever paper, technique or design comes to mind. Don't think about it—just do it. After you're done, analyze the page. What worked? What didn't? Use the things that worked on a "real" page.

There you go—great advice from great scrapbookers. I'm taking their advice to heart and will go a little wild on my next layout, straight lines be darned! ❤

"Matthew"
by Shannon Wolz
Casper, WY

Supplies *Definition and brad:* Making Memories; *Faux wax seal:* Creative Imaginations; *Patterned paper:* 7 Gypsies; *Stamping ink:* ColorBox, Clearsnap; *Embossing powder:* Suze Weinberg; *Computer font:* CK Newsprint, "Fresh Fonts" CD, *Creating Keepsakes; Metallic rubons:* Craf-T Products.

initial it!

Add a hip twist with a trendy font

Items that sport initials are all the rage. Wait! Before you think of the wacky "L" shirt from the old "Laverne and Shirley" sitcom, consider the classic monogram. You can update the look with a trendy font.

While simple serif, sans serif and script fonts add a stylish touch to today's clothing and accessories, they're also terrific fits for scrapbook pages. So are distressed typewriter and grungy stencil fonts. Next time you're eager to try something new, add an initial or monogram to your page. The layout here shows how fun and fabulous this can be! ♥

Renovate the classic monogram for a customized page accent. *Pages by Ali Edwards.* **Supplies** *Textured cardstock:* Bazzill Basics; *Patterned paper:* Rusty Pickle; *Fabric tag:* me & my BIG ideas; *Washers:* Making Memories; *Brads:* www.twopeasinabucket.com; *Computer fonts:* Arial Black, Microsoft Word; Problem Secretary, downloaded from the Internet. *Idea to note:* Ali created the "S" block to repeat the basic look of the alphabet-block patterned paper.

Ready to give initials a try? Consider using brass templates, lettering templates, stickers, rubber stamps, punches, epoxy or acrylic letters, die cuts or computer fonts. Check out offerings from these companies:

◆ All My Memories . . . . *www.allmymemories.com*
◆ Creative Imaginations . . . . *www.cigift.com*
◆ EK Success . . . . *www.eksuccess.com*
◆ Making Memories . . . . *www.makingmemories.com*
◆ Mrs. Grossman's . . . . *www.mrsgrossmans.com*
◆ Sizzix . . . . *www.sizzix.com*

ARTICLE BY LORI FAIRBANKS

ignite your imagination!

Try these fabulous looks for fall

Just because the temperatures are dropping doesn't mean your creativity has to. Let scrapbookers Rhonda Solomon, Julie Turner and Heather Uppencamp inspire you with three innovative techniques that are sure to ignite your imagination.

Work-of-Art Watercolors

Explore your artistic side / by Rhonda Solomon

Watercolor paper by Strathmore
Tube watercolors by Grumbacher
Brushes by Royal

Something about watercolors is special. Is it their transparency, their fluidity or their brilliant hues? I just can't pinpoint it. I *do* know that I love the way watercolors make me feel—like an artist, even though I'm far from it.

Watercolor art isn't a perfect science—it's forgiving. And there's no right or wrong way to do it. All you need is a little information and your own imagination. Here, I'll tell you what you need to get started, then show you some fabulous ways (from backgrounds to frames to accents) to incorporate watercolors into your scrapbooks. With a little inspiration, you'll be creating one-of-a-kind works of art in no time!

GETTING STARTED

Here's what you'll need to get started:

• **Paper.** Pick up a pad of good watercolor paper, like Strathmore Watercolor Cold Press paper (available at craft and art supply stores). It's heavy, durable and acid free, making it an ideal surface for watercolors.

You can also watercolor on cardstock. It will warp slightly when doing washes or plaids, but the cardstock will flatten out after it's been placed in a page protector or under a book for an hour or two.

• **Brushes.** You'll want a few round brushes and a few flat brushes in different sizes. A good liner brush is nice for detail. I like the Red Sable line, but you'll find several good synthetic and nylon brushes that are less expensive and work well. Throw a toothbrush in your watercolor toolbox, too.

• **Paints.** Watercolors come in a variety of forms, such as pencils, tubes and cakes. I've used them all but prefer cake watercolors for their versatility.

You can also choose from student-grade watercolors, which are less expensive, and artist-grade watercolors, which have finer pigments. I generally don't purchase expensive paints; I just look for colors I like. A palette of 12–24 colors is usually plenty. With practice, you'll learn to mix colors to get just the hues you want. It's also a good idea to have a tube of white watercolor on hand to lighten tones.

4 LOVELY LOOKS

Now that you've stocked up on the basic supplies, you're ready to get your brushes wet and get to work. I've included the supplies you'll need for each project, plus step-by-step instructions so you can re-create the looks on your own.

#1 Watercolor Wash

The wash technique is perfect for backgrounds or any time you need a subtle wash of color.

To create a wash:

1. Dilute the watercolor with a fair amount of water.

2. Using a large, flat brush, paint quickly over the surface of the paper in a back-and-forth motion.

3. Let the paint dry.

Figure 1. Add subtle color to title blocks, frames and accents with a watercolor wash. *Pages by Rhonda Solomon.* **Supplies** *Linen cardstock:* Paper Inspirations; *Watercolors:* Grumbacher; *Rubber stamps:* Hot Potatoes (alphabet) and PSX Design (backgrounds); *Stamping ink:* ColorBox, Clearsnap; *Cardstock reinforcements:* Rhonda's own designs; *Square punches:* Family Treasures; *Tags, snaps, eyelets and wire:* Making Memories; *Photo corners:* Boston Int'l; *Pen:* Zig Writer, EK Success; *Other:* Twigs and wire mesh.

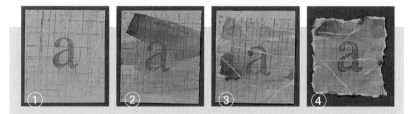

To create the title block in Figure 1:

1. Stamp the background, then stamp the title letters.

2. Apply a rust watercolor wash over the letters.

3. Once the wash is dry, bend and crinkle the paper.

4. Tear the paper into a block and rub with sandpaper. Ink the edges of the block with black ink, then lightly outline the letters with a fine black marker.

To create the layout in Figure 1:

1. Complete the "Cattle Call" title following the steps above.

2. Stamp the chicken wire rubber stamp onto a small strip of paper, then stamp "Our Backyard" over the background. Crinkle the strip and rub it with sandpaper. Apply a cardstock reinforcement (made with two square punches) and attach to a square of wire mesh with wire.

3. Stamp the chicken wire rubber stamp onto a smaller strip of paper, then stamp the date over the background. Crinkle and rub with sandpaper. Place the strip behind the label plate and attach to wire mesh with snaps.

4. To create the photo frame, print out the journaling and apply a rust watercolor wash. Tear the paper into a block, then tear a window for the photo. Crinkle the paper and rub it with sandpaper. Attach eyelets to the photo frame and use wire to connect to the small twigs.

5. Add cardstock reinforcements to the title block and use wire to connect to the larger twig.

6. Stamp backgrounds and letters onto the metal-rimmed tags, then attach them to the wire mesh with snaps and string.

7. Cut photo mats to the desired size and rub edges with black ink. Attach photos to mats with photo corners.

8. Use a small square punch to punch out detail shots, then apply them to the page.

PLAY 1. to partic[...] recreation 2. to parti[...] in a game or sport 3. a child's pastime

smile (smil) to move the tips of one's mouth upward to express pleasure or happiness

treasure (trezh' er) 1. accumulated wealth 2. something of great worth 3. irreplaceable, priceless

LAURA LIVES ACROSS THE STREET. We [...]

APRIL 2003

Figure 2. Sunny watercolored flowers are the perfect accent for a page about playing with friends. *Page by Rhonda Solomon.* **Supplies** *Linen cardstock:* Paper Inspirations; *Watercolors:* Grumbacher; *Alphabet stamps:* Hot Potatoes; *Black stamping ink:* ColorBox, Clearsnap; *Embossing enamel:* Ultra Thick Embossing Enamel, Suze Weinberg; *Definitions:* Making Memories; *Buttons:* Making Memories and Hillcreek Designs; *Computer font:* CK Chemistry, "Fresh Fonts" CD, *Creating Keepsakes; Other:* Vellum envelopes and ribbon.

To create the layout in Figure 2:

1. Adhere photos to the left-hand side of the page.

2. Create the "Giggle" title by stamping and embossing each letter on a block of cardstock. Mat the letters on various shapes and stitch on buttons.

3. Watercolor flowers following the steps below. Mat with coordinating cardstock and rub edges with black ink. Attach two larger flower accents to the front of the vellum envelopes.

4. Insert the "Play" definition in a vellum envelope, then attach it to your page.

5. Print out journaling, cut the paper to size, and rub the edges with black ink. Punch a hole in the top and tie on ribbon. Insert the journaling into a vellum envelope. Remember to cut a slit in the page protector so the journaling block can be removed.

6. Rub the edges of the "Smile" and "Treasure" definitions with black ink, then attach them to the page.

7. Adhere the two remaining flower accents to the page.

#2 Flower Accents

Watercolor flower accents are easy to create and can be modified to fit any layout. Choose your favorite colors and let your brush do the work for you!

To create a flower:

1. Load a round brush with the desired color of paint. Place the brush on the paper and drag out slowly, or apply pressure, then release.

2. Continue painting petals, working from the outside to the center of the flower. Work your way around until you've completed the petals.

3. Paint the flower center with brown watercolor.

4. Using a fine liner brush, add black dots to the brown center. Next, add green stems and a leaf.

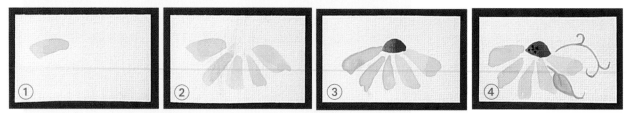

Figure 3. Set off a special photo with a watercolored plaid frame. A light coat of shellac ink adds a hint of shimmer. *Pages by Rhonda Solomon.* **Supplies** *Watercolors:* Sennelier; *Linen cardstock:* Paper Inspirations; *Embossed background paper:* K & Company; *Metal letters:* Making Memories; *Skeletonized leaves:* Black Ink; *Buttons:* Magic Scraps; *Fiber:* Timeless Touches; *Key:* Homestead Collectibles; *Black stamping ink:* ColorBox, Clearsnap; *Photo corners:* Boston Int'l; *Shelf under photo:* Rhonda's own design; *Other:* Mica, shellac ink, ribbon and silk flowers.

To create the layout in Figure 3:

1. Create the plaid frame following the instructions at right.

2. Adhere the frame to burgundy cardstock, then trim the outside and inside edges.

3. Place a photo under the frame. Machine-stitch the outside edges to the background paper with a straight stitch.

4. Use a specialty stitch to machine-stitch a border along the left-hand side of the page.

5. Embellish the frame with metal letters, skeletonized leaves, silk flowers and a button.

6. Stitch buttons on the left-hand and right-hand sides of the frame. Connect them with a strand of fiber that spans the page.

7. Cut cardstock to create a "shelf" to go under your photo. (*Editor's note:* For specific instructions on creating the paper-molding shelf,

see Rhonda's book *Unique Techniques 3* by Pixie Press.) Rub the cardstock lightly with shellac ink, then adhere the cardstock to the embossed background paper.

8. Mat the photo with burgundy cardstock, insert photo corners, and adhere the photo above the "shelf" on embossed background paper.

Add a mica piece over the bouquet.

9. Adhere the invitation to the background by stitching along the top with a specialty stitch. Add a mica piece on top of the invitation.

10. Tie a key to the background with sheer ribbon. Place it on a scrap of plaid cut from the center of the frame.

#3 Plaid Frame

A plaid frame is a beautiful way to set off a special photo. Use muted tones for classy shots or bright colors for a more playful look.

To create the plaid frame in Figure 3:

1. Load a flat brush with burgundy, then paint vertical stripes on white cardstock.

2. When the vertical stripes are dry, load the brush with pink and paint horizontal stripes over the vertical stripes.

3. When the horizontal stripes are dry, load a liner brush with yellow and paint smaller stripes on each side of the large stripes.

4. Trim frame to desired size.

5. Rub frame with shellac ink.

6. Rub edges lightly with black ink.

Figure 4. Muted watercolors dress up a fall-themed rubber stamp, providing the perfect focal point for a seasonal card. *Card by Rhonda Solomon.* **Supplies** *Rubber stamp:* Rubber Monger; *Watercolors:* Grumbacher; *Linen cardstock:* Paper Inspirations; *Other:* Raffia.

#4 Stamped Image

Watercolors add just the right amount of subtle color to a stamped design.

To create the stamped image:

1. Stamp image in black.

2. When the ink has dried, add watercolors with a small brush.

3. Let the paint dry.

To create the card in Figure 4:

1. Cut a piece of dark-brown cardstock to 8½" x 4". Fold the paper in half.

2. Cut strips of rust, light-brown and olive cardstock in varying sizes. Adhere the strips to the front of your card.

3. Punch holes in the top of the front cover and tie a raffia bow.

4. Stamp image in black. When dried, add watercolors and let dry.

5. Mat the stamped image with dark-brown, olive and rust cardstock. Adhere the image on top of the cardstock strips.

Keep track of ideas and techniques in a swatch book that's dressed up with a customized cover.

Supplies *Linen cardstock:* Paper Inspirations; *Watercolors:* Grumbacher, Sennelier and Loew-Cornell; *Metal letters and word, eyelet, snaps and wire:* Making Memories; *Alphabet stamps:* Pixie Press ("by"); *Grapes:* Rhonda's own design; *Stamping ink:* ColorBox, Clearsnap; *Embossing enamel:* Ultra Thick Embossing Enamel, Suze Weinberg; *Pen:* Zig Writer, EK Success; *Other:* Gold brad, metal hook and torn page from a book.

Watercolor Swatch Book

A swatch book is the perfect place to record ideas and techniques. Mine is filled with watercolor patterns and design ideas, and it's small enough that I can take it with me when I need to. The customized cover makes it even more charming to look at.

Following are some additional techniques to try:

• **Create stripes.** Use flat brushes in different sizes to make a few wide stripes of color. Use a liner brush to add small lines of color in between.

• **Add speckles.** Wet a toothbrush and scrub it on your watercolor palette. Holding the toothbrush over cardstock, rub your thumb along the bristles so flecks of paint land on the paper. Practice first—you don't want too much water for this technique.

• **Use a wax crayon or artist's tape.** Create plaids, stripes or swirly designs with a wax crayon or artist's tape, then paint over the design with watercolor. The crayon or tape will preserve the "white" space, leaving your design uncolored. If desired, you can paint over the design with a lighter watercolor.

• **Emboss your design.** Embossing a watercolored design gives it a glossy, finished look. Vellum doesn't have enough texture to absorb watercolor.

ignite your Imagination!

Watercoloring on Vellum

If you want your watercolored design on vellum, simply paint the watercolor on paper and let it dry. Scan the results, then output the electronic image on vellum.

More Watercolor Art

Interested in creating more "wow" looks with watercolors? Get more ideas for backgrounds, frames and titles, accents, speckling and extras in Rhonda Solomon's idea-packed *Watercolors* book by Pixie Press (*www.pixiepress.com*). The book is part of an Idea Bouquet series that also includes *Antique Charm*, *Stitches* and more.

Classic Cracked Enamel

Create a timeless feel / by Heather Uppencamp

You already know what a useful tool a Xyron machine is. But did you know you can use the Xyron leftovers to create a beautiful finish for scrapbook pages? That's right. The release paper—the backing we all toss in the trash—is the perfect surface for creating a cracked enamel that's as versatile as it is lovely. So don't throw away those scraps . . . make gorgeous embellishments instead! Here's how you can create the cracked fall leaf and frame on my layout in Figure 5.

Don't throw away that backing paper.

Figure 5. Create rich cracked enamel by coating Xyron release paper with embossing powder. Bend and crack in places for an aged look. **Supplies** *Patterned paper:* Sharon Ann Collection, Déjà Views, The C-Thru Ruler Co.; *Mesh:* Magenta; *Gold letter stickers:* Class A'Peels, Stampendous!; *Stamping ink:* Dauber Duos, Tsukineko; *Embossing enamel:* Ultra Thick Embossing Enamel, Suze Weinberg; *Fibers:* Fibers By The Yard.

To create the frame:

1. Cut out the frame from the Xyron release paper.

2. Spread a generous amount of ink on the slick side of the frame.

3. Emboss the ink with several layers of gold Ultra Thick Embossing Enamel (UTEE).

Let the enamel cool.

4. Remove the release paper from the frame.

5. Bend and crack the frame. I like to make the same number of cracks on each side so the spacing is even when the frame is reassembled.

6. Adhere each piece with Scrappy Glue.

To create the leaf:

1. Punch a leaf from the Xyron release paper.

2. Evenly spread a generous amount of ink on the slick side of the leaf shape.

3. Sprinkle gold Ultra Thick Embossing Enamel on the leaf and shake off any excess. Heat the UTEE. While it's still very hot, add another layer of UTEE.

Heat again. Repeat this process until you have 3–4 layers of UTEE. Let the enamel cool.

4. Remove the release paper from the back of the leaf. It will peel right off.

5. Over a piece of scrap paper, bend the leaf in two or three places to crack it. The paper will catch any small pieces that fall.

6. Reassemble the leaf on scrap paper so you know where each piece goes.

7. A piece at a time, spread a thin layer of liquid adhesive (I love Scrappy Glue by Magic Scraps) on the back of each piece and glue it down. Leave a small space between the pieces for a mosaic effect.

Not only is the Xyron handy for applying adhesive, you can use the backing paper.

A few helpful hints:

• The release paper is very light and can blow away or curl while embossing. I like to use a small piece of double-stick tape to hold my shapes in place while embossing them. The tape will come off the slick surface easily when you're done.

• When creating larger shapes like the frame shown in Figure 5, emboss a section at a time. In other words, ink and sprinkle UTEE over the whole shape, but heat about two inches at a time. Sprinkle another layer of UTEE over the melted area and shake off any excess. Move to the next 2" section and repeat until you've gone around the frame three times or more.

• Only bend your shape in a few places. Too many cracks will create tiny pieces that are tedious to reassemble.

• Don't be afraid to play with this technique. You've got lots of possibilities!

Ultra Thick Embossing Enamel by Suze Weinberg

Scrappy Glue by Magic Scraps

Wonders with Walnut Ink

Add a warm, earthy look to your creations / by Julie Turner

What could be better for fall pages than the warm, earthy patina of walnut ink? A long-time favorite of artists and calligraphers, walnut ink has become a staple in scrapbookers' toolboxes. The rich brown color creates a dramatic look that's ideal for creating backgrounds, washes, aged looks and more.

Read on to learn the basics of using walnut ink, then find out how I used this versatile product to enhance several of my favorite tag designs.

What Is Walnut Ink?

Walnut ink, made in years past by boiling walnut shells, is a type of ink, not a brand or color. Today it comes in crystal form and is sold by a variety of companies, including 7 Gypsies (*www.7gypsies.com*) and Postmodern Designs (405/321-3176).

How Do I Use Walnut Ink?

Mix one heaping teaspoon of crystals into hot water to create the ink. It's very concentrated, so a little goes a long way. To antique papers and ribbon, you'll need to dilute the ink with additional water so it's one-half or one-quarter of its original strength. Put the diluted ink in a shallow dish and dip tags, paper, envelopes, ribbon and more into the ink. Spread the items on a cookie sheet or waxed paper to dry.

Is It Safe?

The pH of walnut ink is not known. For archival soundness, spray items with Archival Mist by Preservation Technologies (*www.eksuccess.com*) or Make It Acid-Free! by Krylon (*www.krylon.com*). Or, mock the look with similar supplies.

Walnut ink by 7 Gypsies

Gather a variety of interesting supplies to "age" with walnut ink. You can see how they turned out in the samples that follow!

8 Tags Inspired by Autumn

I love to use walnut ink to add a warm, aged look to tags for scrapbook pages, cards and gifts. Here's how to create eight fantastic looks for fall.

Dip patterned and handmade papers in walnut ink for a beautiful aged look.

"Big Leaf" Supplies *Walnut ink:* 7 Gypsies; *Silk embroidery ribbon:* Bucilla; *Hemp cord:* Darice; *Metal eyelet date:* Making Memories; *Other:* Leaf.

To duplicate this easy technique, cut a tag from ivory cardstock and dip it in diluted walnut ink. Or, create a similar effect by brushing the ink on with a sponge brush.

"Mom, Son" Supplies *Walnut ink:* 7 Gypsies; *Metal frame and letters:* Making Memories; *Fiber:* DMC; *Other:* Glass and scrap of bookbinding cloth.

Try crumpling a tag before dipping it into walnut ink. As it dries, the color will settle into the cracks.

"Remember/Dried Flower" Supplies *Walnut ink:* 7 Gypsies; *Embossed paper:* Source unknown; *Silk ribbon:* Bucilla; *Embroidery floss and metal brad:* Making Memories; *Dried flower:* Nature's Pressed; *Other:* Quote from an old book, scrap of bookbinding cloth.

I dipped the embossed paper in a light solution of walnut ink before adding embellishments. I also dipped the ribbon and embroidery floss in the ink. For the best results when dying ribbon, use silk embroidery ribbon.

"Happy Heart Tag" Supplies *Envelope tag:* Ink It!; *Tiny envelope:* Hero Arts; *Walnut ink:* 7 Gypsies; *Heart eyelet and bead chain:* Making Memories; *Crimper:* ScrapWorks; *Charm:* Paper Parachute.

To re-create this look, crumple the large envelope tag and dip it in walnut ink. Dip again for a darker color. Smear the tiny envelope with purple ink, then dip it in walnut ink. If the moisture causes the envelope to become unglued, simply re-glue it.

"Tiny Photos" Supplies *Walnut ink:* 7 Gypsies; *Snap tape:* Dritz.

To create the mottled effect on this tag, dip the tag in a darker dilution of ink, then use a squirt bottle to spritz the tag with water. The ink will repel the water, forming interesting patterns.

You can also fill the squirt bottle with ink and spritz the surface of the tag.

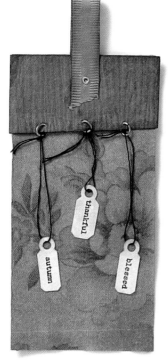

"Thankful" Supplies *Walnut ink:* 7 Gypsies; *Patterned paper:* Daisy D's; *Small tags:* American Tag Co.; *Eyelet:* Making Memories; *Embroidery floss:* DMC; *Other:* Jump rings and ribbon.

Dipping patterned and handmade papers in walnut ink will give them a beautiful aged look. Not all papers accept walnut ink well; experiment with scraps to find what works best.

"Silver Bars" Supplies *Walnut ink, metal bars and jump ring:* 7 Gypsies; *Eyelets and fibers:* Making Memories.

To duplicate this look, cut a pink piece of cardstock into a tag. Spritz it with water, crumple it, and iron flat. When dipped in walnut ink, the tag will turn a lovely brown.

"Dried Leaf" Supplies *Walnut ink:* 7 Gypsies; *Green ink:* ColorBox, Clearsnap; *Dried leaf:* Nature's Pressed; *Eyelet:* Making Memories; *Embroidery floss:* DMC.

Tone down a bright color with walnut ink. Here, I smeared bright-green ink across a tag and dipped it in walnut ink. To make the stitched border, I used my sewing machine, without thread, to zigzag holes across the top and bottom of the tag. Then I went back and hand-stitched the pattern with thread. ♥

Ooh-Aah-Oh!

ARTISTIC ACCENTS WITH THE WOW FACTOR

Ever walk through an art exhibit and just marvel at the talent? My sister-in-law and I browsed a gallery recently during a Saturday shopping excursion. (I'm looking for a prominent art accent for my living room.) The muted lighting and soothing music were relaxing, but what stood out most was the incredible artistry on exhibit. It inspired me to want to create something as lovely on my scrapbook pages.

Recently, we asked our 2003 Hall of Fame winners to show us some of their best artistic accents. As the accents poured in, I oohed and aahed and exclaimed to my coworkers, "Quick! You've just got to see these accents." (It's a wonder we got any work done!) We hope you are as impressed with the following accents as we were. Our Hall of Famers' talent is truly inspiring. *by Lanna Carter*

i look at my daughter and i believe...

[be´·lieve]
to have faith in

discover

explore

paradise

SPRING
memories

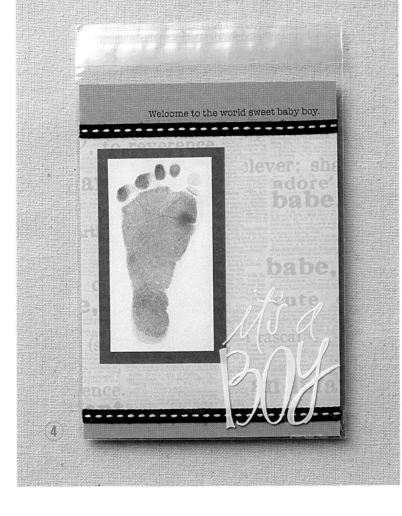

Welcome to the world sweet baby boy.

it's a BOY

HAPPY
ASSORTED GOLD EYEN
APY I NEED RETAIL THERA

① "BELIEVE"
by Leslie Lightfoot
Stirling, ON, Canada

Supplies *Patterned papers:* KI Memories; *Buttons:* Laura Ashley, EK Success; *Definition, frame, staples and ribbon:* Making Memories; *Walnut ink:* 7 Gypsies; *Rubber stamp:* Inkadinkado; *Stamping ink:* Memories, Stewart Superior Corporation; *Computer font:* Dutch 801, downloaded from the Internet.

② "DISCOVER"
by Jamie Waters
South Pasadena, CA

Supplies *Patterned paper, bubble words and metal holders:* Li'l Davis Designs; *Mesh:* Magic Mesh, Avant Card; *Rub-ons:* Making Memories; *Other:* Twine and tag.

③ "SPRING"
by Jenni Bowlin
Mt. Juliet, TN

Supplies *Stickers:* Magenta; *Bookplate:* Li'l Davis Designs; *Mini brads:* American Tag Company; *Letter stamp:* Stampers Anonymous; *Stamping ink:* StazOn, Tsukineko; *Other:* Transparency.

④ "IT'S A BOY"
by Ali Edwards
Creswell, OR

Supplies *Envelope:* Deluxe Designs; *Patterned paper:* 7 Gypsies; *Textured cardstock:* Bazzill Basics; *Rub-ons:* Making Memories; *Computer font:* American Typewriter, downloaded from the Internet; *Ribbon:* me & my BIG ideas. *Idea to note:* Ali adhered the rub-ons to the outside of the envelope, then slipped the card inside.

⑤ "RETAIL THERAPY"
by Terrie McDaniel
League City, TX

Supplies *Textured cardstock:* Bazzill Basics; *Patterned papers:* Legacy (collage) and 7 Gypsies (script); *Purse die cut:* Deluxe Designs; *Conchos and letters:* Scrapworks; *Label tape:* Dymo; *Other:* Fibers and stamping ink. *Idea to note:* Terrie changed the pink die cut to black with stamping ink.

⑥ "ARTIST"
by Nichol Magouirk
Dodge City, KS

Supplies *Patterned paper:* Chatterbox; *Metal accents and copper plate:* Global Solutions; *Definition sticker, rub-ons, metal-rimmed tags and staples:* Making Memories; *Acrylic paint:* Delta Technical Coatings; *Letter stamps:* Ma Vinci Reliquary; *Stamping ink:* Memories, Stewart Superior Corporation; *Other:* Thread.

⑦ "TRAVEL JOURNAL"
by Sara Tumpane
Grayslake, IL

Supplies *Clay:* Sculpey and Prêmo; *Letter stamps:* Barnes & Noble (title) and Club Scrap ("The journey…"); *Stamping ink:* StazOn and Brilliance, Tsukineko; *Eyelets:* Making Memories; *Pasta machine:* USArtQuest; *Other:* Hemp. *Ideas to note:* Sara rolled her clay with a pasta machine. She pressed sandpaper into the flat clay for her texture. Last, Sara glued the eyelets into the clay before baking it.

⑨

⑧ **"OUR FAMILY VACATION"**
by Loni Stevens
Pleasant Grove, UT

Supplies *Photo tag:* Cloud 9 Designs;
Patterned paper: Design Originals; *Metal numbers, washers, rub-on and eyelet:*
Making Memories; *Metal word phrase:* Li'l Davis Designs; *Stencil template:* Helix; *Acrylic paint:* Delta Technical Coatings; *Stamping ink:* Ranger Industries; *Other:* Silk flowers, mini buttons, thread, ribbon, twine, denim and mini Scrabble tiles. *Ideas to note:* Loni inked the patterned-paper edges of her "A". She used Li'l Davis Designs' Li'l Stitcher template as a guide while piercing holes around the perimeter of the cutout opening.

⑨ **"TINY TOES"**
by Karen Russell
Grants Pass, OR

Supplies *Labels:* Heart and Home Collectables, Melissa Frances; *Metal corner:* Embellish It; *Walnut ink:* 7 Gypsies; *Other:* Eyelets, safety pin, staples, lace and shoelace. *Ideas to note:* Karen dyed her shoelace with walnut ink for a vintage look. She created her tag from a large label.

⑩ "THE PERFECT PAIR"
by Julie Scattaregia
Carmel, IN

Supplies *Eyelets:* Agence Pierre Grenier, Inc.; *Rub-ons, metal letters, ribbon and oval clip:* Making Memories; *Woven labels:* me & my BIG ideas; *Stamping ink:* Close To My Heart; *Charms:* The Card Connection and Making Memories; *Transfer paper:* Avery; *Other:* Canvas, burlap and lace. *Ideas to note:* Julie used canvas as her tag background. She transferred the playing-card images with iron-on transfer paper. Julie sanded the eyelets for an aged look.

⑪ "CONSTANT COMPANIONS"
by Faye Morrow Bell
Charlotte, NC

Supplies *Hot foil pen and silver foil:* Staedtler; *Twill tape:* Wright's; *Conchos:* Scrapworks; *Computer font:* Typist, downloaded from the Internet; *Other:* Buckle.

⑫ "MAJOR LEAGUE"
by Vanessa Reyes
Lakeport, CA

Supplies *Patterned paper, ribbon and thread:* me & my BIG ideas; *Chalk:* Craf-T Products; *Other:* Brads. *Idea to note:* Vanessa threaded her ribbon strips through the holes she made for the brads, then tied them at the bottom of the mat.

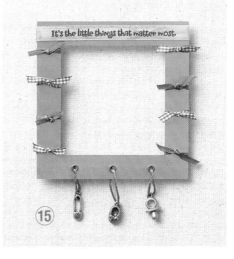

It's the little things that matter most.

⑮

---

⑬ **"YOUR BIG HEART"**
by Jennifer Bester
Reading, MA

Supplies *Circle punch:* Marvy Uchida; *Label, ribbon and thread:* me & my BIG ideas; *Heart accent:* Meri Meri; *Letter stamps:* PSX Design; *Stamping ink:* Marvy Matchables, Marvy Uchida.

⑭ **"ENJOY VACATION"**
by Tracy Miller
Fallston, MD

Supplies *Patterned paper, ribbon, tag and labels:* me & my BIG ideas; *Dimensional letter stickers:* Li'l Davis Designs; *Stamping ink:* ColorBox, Clearsnap; *Other:* Flat-head eyelet.

⑮ **"IT'S THE LITTLE THINGS"**
by Joy Uzarraga
Clarendon Hills, IL

Supplies *Ribbon:* Lavish Lines (quote), C.M. Offray & Son (pink) and unknown (gingham); *Metal frame:* Making Memories; *Eyelets:* Doodlebug Design; *Charms:* Watch Us, Inc.; *Embroidery floss:* DMC; *Chalk:* Craf-T Products. *Idea to note:* Joy chalked her quote ribbon to match her color scheme.

⑯ **"LOVE NOTES"**
by Lisa Russo
Oswego, IL

Supplies *Typewriter keys:* Magic Scraps; *Letter stamps:* PSX Design; *Envelope:* Magenta; *Rubber stamps:* Limited Edition Rubber Stamps, Renaissance Art Stamps, Hampton Arts, Hero Arts, Inkadinkado, Stampers Anonymous and Penny Black; *Stamping ink:* ColorBox, Clearsnap; Memories, Stewart Superior Corporation; VersaColor, Tsukineko; *Embossing powder:* Hero Arts; *Ephemera:* me & my BIG ideas; Nostalgiques, EK Success; *Clasp:* 7 Gypsies. *Idea to note:* Lisa stamped the letters on the typewriter keys, then embossed them with clear embossing powder.

⑰ **"WE ARE FRIENDS"**
by Amie Lloyd
Broken Arrow, OK

Supplies *Patterned paper:* KI Memories; *Definition sticker, metal letters:* Making Memories; *Fibers:* Fibers By The Yard; *Metal rod, typewriter key and watch part:* 7 Gypsies; *Key charm:* Jolee's By You, Sticko for EK Success; *Paper tiles:* Creative Imaginations; *Transparency:* Altered Pages; *Bead:* Magic Scraps; *Other:* Slide holder and heart charm.

(18) "USA"
by Kelly Anderson
Tempe, AZ

Supplies *Vellum images:* Scrappy's; *Safety pins and dog tag:* Li'l Davis Designs; *Bubble letters:* Sonnets, Creative Imaginations; *Star charms:* Beads Galore; *Heart punch:* Emagination Crafts; *Scrap metal:* Once Upon a Scribble; *Fibers:* On The Surface and Special Effects; *Other:* Tag, atlas paper and penny.

(19) "READ"
by Maya Opavska
Redmond, WA

Supplies *Textured cardstock:* Hanko Designs; *Rubber stamps:* Turtle Press; *Stamping ink:* Stampin' Up! (black); Fabrico (gray), Tsukineko; *Pen:* Marvy Uchida; *Computer images:* The Vintage Workshop; *Snaps:* Making Memories; *Other:* Transparency and thread. *Idea to note:* Maya printed her images on a transparency, then anchored it to her tag with a sewing machine. Note how it works as a pocket for a smaller tag.

(20) "DREAM"
by Dawn Brookey
La Crescenta, CA

Supplies *Patterned paper:* Li'l Davis Designs (sewing) and unknown (blue floral); *Beads:* JewelCraft; *Crystal lacquer:* Glossy Accents, Ranger Industries; *Dream label:* Scrappy Chic, me & my BIG ideas; *Keyhole:* Li'l Davis Designs; *Adhesive:* Photo Tape, 3M; Metal Glue, Li'l Davis Designs; *Tags:* Making Memories (metal-rimmed) and Dawn's own design (large); *Other:* Library envelope, silk ribbon and circle tag. *Idea to note:* Dawn removed the paper from the metal-rimmed tag and replaced it with patterned paper. She covered the surface with crystal lacquer, then set the beads in it.

(21) "CRYSTAL TAG"
by Heidi Stepanova
Centralia, IL

Supplies *Patterned paper:* Anna Griffin; *Ribbon:* me & my BIG ideas (green) and C.M. Offray & Son; *Crystals:* Mrs. Grossman's; *Silver leafing pen:* Krylon; *Daisy corners:* Making Memories; *Acrylic paint:* Delta Technical Coatings.

(22) "THIS IS ME NOW"
by Tracie Smith
Smithtown, NY

Supplies *Stamping ink:* Vintage Ink, Ranger Industries; *Library cardholder:* The Inkpad; *Metal letters:* Making Memories; *Embossed paper:* K & Company; *Acrylic frame and black ink:* Krystal Kraft; *Script stamp:* A Stamp in the Hand; *Embossing enamel:* Suze Weinberg; *Ribbon:* me & my BIG ideas; *Craft wire:* Artistic Wire Ltd.; *Acrylic paint:* Americana, DecoArt; *Pen:* Zig Millennium, EK Success; *Adhesive:* Glue Dots International; *Other:* Thread. *Ideas to note:* Tracie rubbed stamping ink over the surface of the library cardholder, then spritzed it with water to create the spotted look. She also rubbed an inkpad over her embossed paper. Tracie stamped a script stamp on the frame, then embossed it with embossing enamel.

㉓ "BABY CAMERON"
by Alison Beachem
San Diego, CA

Supplies *Patterned paper and cutouts:*
Chronicles, Two Busy Moms; *File folder:*
Pinecone Press; *Embroidery floss:* DMC;
Letter stamps: Rubber Stampede; *Other:*
Stamping ink and foam tape. *Idea to
note:* Alison adhered an extra card to the
inside of her file folder, which accommo-
dates three more pictures. ♥

★ CREATING TILE LETTERS ★

I love the look of these little tile letters (Figure 1). Whether you use them for your title, subtitle or even as photo captions, they add a beautiful touch to layouts. Best of all, they're easy to make—just follow these steps:

❶ Place your letter stickers on cardstock. Remember to leave enough space between the letters.

❷ Cut the cardstock into squares. When cutting around each letter, make the tiles as large or small as you like. Tiles can be cut the same size, or try cutting letters into different-sized squares.

❸ Chalk around the edges of each tile letter. After chalking the edges, use your finger to blend the chalk inward. You can also use ink to sponge edges for an antique look.

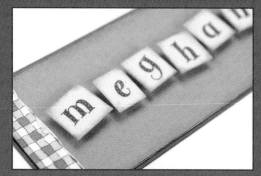

❹ Place foam squares under each tile letter and place it on your layout or tag. This will give your tile letters a dimensional look.

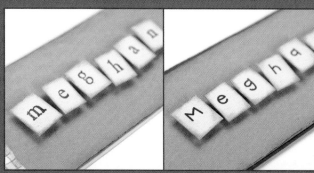

Figure 1. Create tile letters with computer fonts, stickers or rubber stamps. **Supplies** *Patterned paper:* O'Scrap!, Imaginations, Inc.; *Computer font:* CK Handprint, "The Best of Creative Lettering" CD Combo, *Creating Keepsakes; Rubber stamps:* PSX Design; *Stamping ink:* Splendor, Tsukineko; *Letter stickers:* me & my BIG ideas; *Fibers:* Rubba Dub Dub, Art Sanctum; *Circle punch:* Family Treasures; *Foam squares:* Therm O Web; *Tags:* Katherine's own design.

Variation: For more fun looks with this technique, try using rubber stamp alphabets, computer fonts or your own handwriting!

—*Katherine Brooks*
Gilbert, AZ

Figure 1. Use chalk and dry-embossed lines to create a cardstock photo mat that looks like a frame. *Pages by Leah Fung.* **Supplies** *Patterned paper:* K & Company; *Elastic:* 7 Gypsies; *Eyelets and brads:* Making Memories; *Paper flowers:* Hirschberg, Schutz & Co.; *Ribbon:* Close To My Heart; *Chalk:* Craf-T Products; *Corrugated paper:* DMD, Inc.; *Computer font:* Times New Roman, Microsoft Word; CK Chemistry, "Fresh Fonts" CD, *Creating Keepsakes; Other:* Charm, bookplate and suede paper.

Dry-embossed Frames

My scrapbooking style is influenced by home interiors. Here's how you can create cardstock photo mats that look like picture frames (Figure 1):

❶ Cut a frame out of cardstock. Rub both sides with waxed paper (this helps the stylus glide across the cardstock).

❷ Place the frame over a metal ruler, leaving ¼" of the ruler exposed.

❸ Using an embossing stylus, emboss a line along the edge of the frame. Leave a ¼" margin on each side. Flip the frame over to show the front side.

❹ Place the frame, front side up, on the metal ruler. Leave ⅛" of the ruler exposed. Emboss the inside edges of the frame, leaving a ⅛" margin on each side.

❺ To create the mat, cut a smaller cardstock frame. Measure it so only ⅛" of the smaller frame will show from behind the larger frame.

❻ Adhere the mat to the back of the frame, then chalk the front of the frame with black and brown chalks.

❼ Adhere your photo behind the mat, then mount the entire piece on acid-free cardboard (or foam tape) to add dimension.

Variation: Emboss diagonal lines from inside corners to outside corners to create a mitered look

—*Leah Fung, San Diego, CA*

friend-ship ('ship), n. intimacy;
united with affection or esteem;
mutual attachment; good will.

J O Y

holidays
2003

9

GREAT GIFT ALBUMS

· Create a mini masterpiece ·

December—it's that time of year when gift giving abounds and many of us scramble for last-minute gifts for loved ones. Have you considered a gift album? It's a great way to spotlight a person, express yourself artistically, or create a unique piece that can be enjoyed by young and old. Here are nine album ideas to inspire you.

by Becky Higgins

For my mother's 55th birthday (sorry to divulge that, Mom!) I made a list of 55 things I love about her. I found relevant pictures and put them together in a book that she adores. Does someone in your life deserve to know all the "little" things you love about him or her? Consider doing a joint gift—ask a group of people to contribute to your project.

Make a list of things you love about someone and scrapbook that list in a stylishly decorated album.

Supplies *Album:* Making Memories; *Patterned paper:* K•I Memories; *Stickers:* Creative Imaginations; *Brads:* Lasting Impressions for Paper; *Pen and apron accents:* Jolee's Boutique, Sticko by EK Success; *Computer fonts:* Century Gothic, Microsoft Word; CK Cursive (subtitle), "The Art of Creative Lettering" CD; CK Tipsy (numbers), "Creative Clips & Fonts" CD, *Creating Keepsakes;* *Charm:* Artistic Expressions; *Silver-rimmed tag, safety pin, hinge and metal letters:* Making Memories; *Words on fabric strips:* me & my BIG ideas; *Other:* Ribbon and staples.

2 "Seasons" and "Joy"

All you need to create these quick, custom albums is cardstock, a Roll-a-bind and fun die cuts and accents.

Make custom albums in a snap with cardstock and a Roll-a-bind.

Supplies *Die cuts:* Ellison and Sizzix; *Patterned paper:* The Paper Patch; *Adhesive:* Xyron; *Stickers:* Mrs. Grossman's; *Metal letters:* Making Memories; *Pop dots:* All Night Media; *Beaded metal chain:* Ellison: *Ribbon:* C.M. Offray & Son; *Vellum:* Paper Adventures: *Gold paper:* Daler Rowney; *Binding disks:* Roll-a-bind.

When Shayna's children, Brynn and Ethan, requested a book about colors, she was prepared for the challenge. She loves watching her children enjoy the book time after time. Each layout features a color and coordinating items (represented with stickers and other colorful accents).

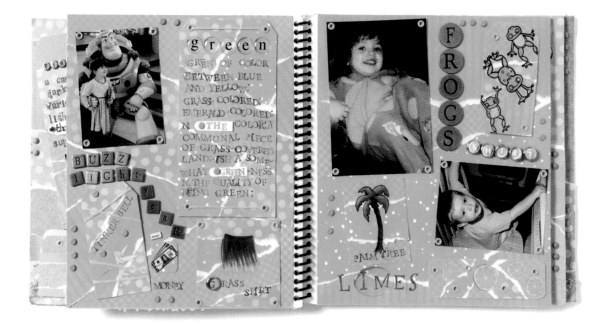

Supplies *Album:* All My Memories; *Patterned paper, brads and buttons:* All My Memories; *Metal letters, frames and clear 3-D stickers:* Making Memories; *Flower letter stickers:* Creative Imaginations; *Letter stamps:* Hero Arts; *Fibers:* All My Memories and Making Memories; *Eyelets:* Creative Impressions and All My Memories; *Mini envelopes:* DMD, Inc.; *Stickers:* Sandylion, Paper House Productions, Mrs. Grossman's and All My Memories; *Conchos and slide frame:* ScrapWorks. *Idea to note:* Shayna trimmed the album from its original 8½" x 11" size.

This color concept book will stimulate a child's senses and grab an adult's attention.

Debbie wanted to create a "He Said, She Said" album for her parents' 53rd wedding anniversary. She enlisted the help of her niece Erin, and the two chose a gated-journal approach. Because a gated journal is spiral bound on two sides, it provides an ideal format to post a question on the center page, then include "he said" comments on a left-hand page and "she said" comments on a right-hand page.

The parents were given the following 10 questions and asked to answer them without consulting each other:

1. Which words would you use to describe your spouse?
2. What do you remember from the first time you two met? (Time, place, clothing and more)
3. What attracted you to him or her? How has that changed now?
4. How many children did each of you want?
5. Where did each of you want to live?
6. What are this person's quirks or pet peeves?
7. In detail, what was your wedding day like?
8. What was it like to meet his or her family for the first time?
9. What are the best of times you remember?
10. What are the worst of times you remember?

While some of the answers were identical, others were humorously different. This album would make a great gift for a newlywed couple.

Two gated-journal tips:

1. To get the "three pages across," start off with a couple of lead pages.

2. Number your pages lightly in pencil and create a corresponding list of what goes on each page front and back.

Supplies *Album:* 7 Gypsies; *Patterned papers:* 7 Gypsies, Anna Griffin, Daisy D's and The Paper Company; *Photo turns and twill tape:* 7 Gypsies; *Brads:* Art Brads; *Clear 3-D stickers:* Making Memories; *Mini frames:* Nunn Design; *Ribbon:* May Arts; *Adhesive:* Perfect Paper Adhesive, USArtQuest; *Rubber stamps:* Limited Edition Rubber Stamps, Stampers Anonymous and Uptown Design Co.

Ask a couple certain questions, then compile the answers in a "He Said, She Said" gift album.

My childhood best friend, Lydia, recently visited and, as usual, we reminisced about our fondest memories. We laughed hard as we flipped through pictures of seriously bad hair, bad taste and fun times. It only made sense to compile some of our favorite photos and memories (including the embarrassing ones) into a gift album. I created two albums—one for each of us—so we can relive these memories time and time again.

Collect favorite pictures for an album that chronicles a lasting friendship.

Supplies *Album:* Maude Asbury; *Circle punches:* Family Treasures (large) and EK Success (small); *Computer fonts:* Metalic Avacado, downloaded from *www.free-typewriter-fonts.com*; CK Regal, "Fresh Fonts" CD, *Creating Keepsakes*; *Album tag:* Making Memories; *Definition:* FoofaLa.

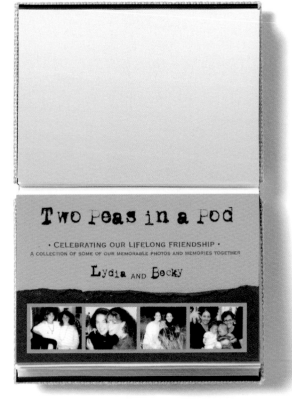

To keep the memories of a child's school year in one place, make a mini album complete with statistics, highlights, papers and artwork. Kellene made this as a gift for her preschooler, Quade. Consider creating a gift album for your child's teacher. This requires some advance planning, so now's the time to think about it. For example, Alyssa Allgaier of Dublin, Ireland, made an album for her daughter's teacher. Alyssa included a page for each child, complete with a photograph and a note of appreciation for the teacher.

Idea to note:

Kellene bound several CD holders with a belt to create this thick album.

Supplies *Album:* CD holders from Pinecone Press; *Tag:* DMD, Inc.; *Patterned paper:* Creative Imaginations; *Metal bookplate:* Magic Scraps; *Metallic rub-ons:* Craf-T Products; *Rubber stamps:* PSX Design and Hero Arts; *Stamping ink:* Clearsnap; *Embossing powder:* Ranger Industries; *Fibers:* Funky Fibers and Timeless Treasures; *Conchos and letters:* ScrapWorks; *Pencil:* Provo Craft; *Pencil design:* EK Success; *Crayon sticker:* Jolee's by You, Sticko by EK Success; *Craft wire:* Artistic Wire Ltd.; *Letter beads:* Westrim Crafts; *Metal letter:* Making Memories; *Metal word:* Scrap-Ease; *Paints:* FolkArt; *Clear spray (on cover):* Krylon; *Other:* Mini composition books.

Compile school memories, artwork and other memorabilia into an album that's perfect for small hands.

"Who Loves Hayden" ALBUM BY MELANIE SOVEREEN

For her nephew Hayden's second birthday, Melanie (a.k.a. "Aunt Mel") made this creatively interactive book. To ensure that Hayden could handle it without limits, Melanie laminated the pages, then had the album spiral-bound.

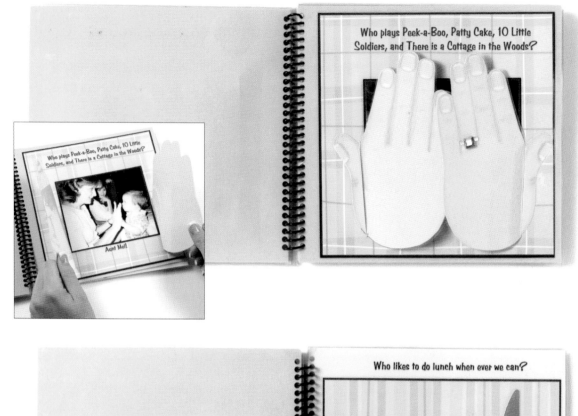

Who plays Peek-a-Boo, Patty Cake, 10 Little Soldiers, and There is a Cottage in the Woods?

Who likes to do lunch when ever we can?

Supplies *Patterned paper:* K•I Memories; *Black letters:* ScrapYard 329; *Heart accent and frame:* Cock-A-Doodle Design; *Elmo designs:* Colorbök; *Hand and food designs:* Melanie's own designs; *Gem:* Westrim Crafts; *Colored pencils:* Prismacolor, Sanford; *Chalk:* Craf-T Products; *Brads:* All My Memories; *Silverware:* Accu-Cut Systems.

Children love interactive books with playful pictures and bright designs.

Amy created a brag book for her mother that includes photos of all six grandchildren. The album moves between her mother's coffee table and purse. Amy made a similar portable brag book of her own family.

To create a "brag book" album, cut sheets of 12" x 12" cardstock in half, stack several sheets together, and hand-stitch them. Amy covered the books with patterned paper (it wraps around to the inside cover), then used Modge Podge to coat it for extra durability. The inside pages have torn edges and are embellished with walnut ink.

Who wouldn't love to carry a family brag book?

Supplies *Walnut ink:* Postmodern Design; *Patterned papesr:* Daisy D's (floral), Pebbles, Inc. (striped) and All My Memories (tiny floral); *Tags:* American Tag Company; *Buttons, eyelets, brads, metal words and letters:* Making Memories; *Vellum:* Paper Adventures; *Rubber stamp:* Close To My Heart; *Embossing enamel:* Suze Weinberg; *Computer font:* CK Heritage, "Creative Clips & Fonts" CD, *Creating Keepsakes.*

9 Small Albums to Hold Your Big Ideas

When creating a gift album, consider these popular offerings. Check your local scrapbook store, or visit the companies' web sites for more information.

MY LEGACY AND SIMPLE LEGACY BY CLOSE TO MY HEART

These postbound albums hold 6" x 6" pages and come in a handful of solid colors.

Web site: *www.closetomyheart.com*
Phone: 888/655-6552

LITTLE KEEPERS BY WE R MEMORY KEEPERS

These postbound albums feature a window on the cover, coordinating ribbon, and 10 designs.

Web site: *www.weronthenet.com*
Phone: 877/742-5937

THE PERFECT SCRAPBOOK BY COLORBÖK

Available in 10 colors, these post-bound albums boast a monochro-matic, designer-style inside cover.

Web site: *www.colorbok.com*
Phone: 734/426-5300

SCRAP ARTISTRY

Choose from postbound albums in 31 designs. Eight albums feature a window in their cover.

Web site: *www.scrapartistry.com*
Phone: 800/688-7367

PERFECT FIT ALBUM BY MAKING MEMORIES

Designed to hold 6" x 6" pages, these washable linen albums come in 12 colors.

Web site: *www.makingmemories.com*
Phone: 800/286-5263

ANNA GRIFFIN

These elegant six-ring binders (each with a ribbon) hold 6" x 6" pages and come in 16 designs.

Web site: *www.annagriffin.com*
Phone: 888/817-8170

Red
HOT!

14 layout ideas that sizzle with creativity

I'll bet you thought you had this article pegged when you read the title. You probably expected our annual Valentine's Day "tribute to love" article. True, we've included a few layouts about love, and a few more include the color red. But our other pages share something else in common. They radiate creative heat—they're hot!

So, dig out a cool summer outfit and pour an ice-cold glass of lemonade. Your temperature may rise as you absorb the energy from these vibrant pages, exciting techniques and passion-inspiring products.

by Lori Fairbanks

Red-Hot Pages

Red is a power color! Use it on your pages to create warmth, showcase a bold design or make a statement.

"Destiny"
by Kimberly Kwan
Scottsdale, AZ

Supplies *Patterned papers:* 7 Gypsies; Chronicles, Two Busy Moms, Deluxe Designs; *Textured cardstock and mulberry paper:* Bazzill Basics; *Rub-on words and square clip:* Making Memories; *Mini brads:* Lost Art Treasures; *Letter cutouts:* Paper Pizazz; *Conchos:* Magic Scraps; *Letter stickers:* Nostalgiques (typewriter), EK Success; Chronicles (red), Two Busy Moms, Deluxe Designs; *Computer fonts:* CK Constitution, "Fresh Fonts" CD, *Creating Keepsakes;* Walrod, downloaded from the Internet; *Other:* Transparency, fibers and a handkerchief from Kimberly's grandmother.

"Adventure"
by Christine Brown
Hanover, MN

Supplies *Patterned papers:* Mustard Moon (black stripe) and The Paper Patch (red); *Computer font:* 2Peas Hot Chocolate, downloaded from *www.twopeasinabucket.com;* *Stamping ink:* Brilliance, Tsukineko (white and brown); Stampendous! (black); *Definition sticker, letter charms, photo corners and eyelets:* Making Memories;

Letter stickers: Shotz and Sonnets, Creative Imaginations; *Circle clips:* Clipiola.

Idea to note: Christine crumpled, stamped, sanded and sponged her patterned paper and stickers with brown ink to create an aged look.

"ABC of Me"

by Ngaire Bartlam
Brisbane, QLD,
Australia

Supplies *Patterned papers:* Sarah Lugg, The Paper Company (daisies and postcard); Karen Foster Design (crackle); 7 Gypsies (text); *Letter stickers, faux wax seals and heart tag:* Sonnets, Creative Imaginations; *Stamping ink:* Art Cube (red); StazOn, Tsukineko (black); *Letter stamps:* Hero Arts, PSX Design and Wordsworth; *Letter cutouts and silver hearts:* FoofaBets, FoofaLa; *Frames and bookplate:* Collections; *Rubber stamps:* Hero Arts; *Other:* Postage stamps, gold beads, tags, fibers, buttons and brads.

"Loved Too, Too Much"

by Vanessa Spady
Virginia Beach, VA

Supplies *Textured cardstock:* Bazzill Basics; *Corrugated paper:* DMD, Inc.; *Vellum:* Susan Branch, Colorbök (flower hearts) and unknown (white hearts); *Rubber stamps:* Rubber Stampede, Susan Branch, Plaid Enterprises and Stampin' Up!; *Letter cutouts:* FoofaBets, FoofaLa; Paper Pizazz (typewriter letters) *Letter stickers:* Mary Engelbreit, Creative Imaginations; *Stamping ink:* Adirondack, Ranger Industries; *Pen:* Slick Writer, American Crafts; *Ribbon:* C.M. Offray & Son; *Typewriter words:* 7 Gypsies; *Heart clips:* Making Memories; *Bookplate:* Two Peas in a Bucket; *Glue dots:* Glue Dots International; *Slide:* Lifetime Moments.

Red-Hot Techniques

Rub-ons, twill tape, walnut ink—they're all the rage. Here are five techniques that use these ultra-hot products.

Page by Jennifer McGuire

Watercolor over clear embossing powder for a beautiful resist effect.

Supplies *Rubber stamps:* Hero Arts and Wordsworth; *Embossing powder:* Hero Arts; *Metal number:* Making Memories; *Stamping ink:* Memories, Stewart Superior Corporation; VersaMark, Tsukineko; *Fibers:* Rubba Dub Dub, Art Sanctum; *Dominos:* Two Peas in a Bucket; *Computer font:* 2Peas Quirky, downloaded from *www.twopeasinabucket.com;* Other: Watercolor paper and a game piece.

Page by Barbara Schipplock

Apply word rub-ons to shrink film for a stylish look.

Supplies *Textured cardstock:* Bazzill Basics; *Patterned papers:* 7 Gypsies; Sonnets, Creative Imaginations; K & Company; Daisy D's; *Photo corners, metal word and rub-ons:* Making Memories; *Elastic and typewriter words:* 7 Gypsies; *Embossing enamel:* Opals, Pipe Dreamink; *Circle clips:* Clipiola; *Eyelets:* Extreme Eyelets, Creative Imaginations; *Letter stamps:* PSX Design; *Glue dots:* Glue Dots International; *Label tape:* Dymo; *Other:* Shrink plastic, transparency, ribbon, fibers, string, buttons, colored pencils and bead chain.

technique

Sensational Shrink Film

I love the versatility of shrink film. Here's how you can use it with rub-ons:

❶ Sand one side of clear shrink film to give it a coarse finish. (This helps the rub-ons stick.) Using the burnishing stick provided, rub words onto the film.

❷ Color in the words with colored pencils.

❸ Punch a hole if you want to use the film as a tag. Remember: The hole will also shrink when you heat the film. I used a circle punch so the hole was fairly large.

❹ Heat the shrink film according to the package instructions.
Tip: The film will curl as it shrinks if you use a heat gun. I used a wooden rubber-stamp base to press the film flat once I liked the size and shape.
Variation: Try this technique with a photo. Sand one side of a sheet of white shrink film. Set your inkjet printer to the "transparency" setting and print a photo onto the shrink film. It will be wet and blotchy at first, so don't touch the ink. Heat the shrink film, then apply two layers of clear embossing powder to set the ink.

—*Barbara Schipplock, Manly West, QLD, Australia*

Red-Hot Techniques

Tag by Jennifer McGuire.

For a different look, apply walnut ink over clear embossed images.

Supplies *Rubber stamps and embossing powder:* Hero Arts; *Embossing ink:* VersaMark, Tsukineko; *Walnut ink:* 7 Gypsies; *Buttons:* Doodlebug Design; *Other:* Beads, ribbon and rickrack. *Ideas to note:* Jennifer cut three tags of varying lengths. After embellishing the tags, she sewed the top of the tags together, then added ribbon, rickrack and beads.

technique

Simply Irresistible

Did you know clear embossing powder and watercolors work well together? This is one of my favorite techniques! Here's how you can easily get this great look:

❶ Stamp your designs with clear pigment ink, then heat emboss the images with clear embossing powder. For my "Eight" layout on page 106, I used watercolor paper, but this technique also looks great on cardstock.

❷ Apply a heavy coat of watercolor paint over the embossed images. This creates a better contrast for the resist effect. Dab away the excess paint. *Variation:* Give this technique a vintage twist by using walnut ink, like I did on my "XOXO" tag.

—*Jennifer McGuire, Cincinnati, OH*

Apply art-masking fluid or rub-ons to your page before watercoloring—both will resist the paint.

Supplies *Watercolor paper:* Canson; *White word rub-ons:* Making Memories; *Masking fluid:* Winsor & Newton; *Snowflake buttons:* Dress It Up, Jesse James & Co.; *Vellum:* The Paper Company; *Computer font:* 2Peas Chicken Shack, downloaded from www.twopeasinabucket.com; *Other:* Ribbon and mittens.

technique

More Irresistible Techniques

I like the artsy look of resist techniques. Here are two easy methods to create this look:

• Apply white letter rub-ons to watercolor paper, then apply your paint. The paint doesn't adhere to the rub-ons, so it looks like you printed directly on the paper. Remove any excess paint drops from the letters with a fine-tipped cotton swab.

Tip: For a cleaner look, apply the rub-ons with a stylus instead of the burnishing stick that comes in the packaging.

• Create your own words or images using art masking fluid. (I drew check boxes on my layout.) After the paint dries, remove the masking fluid by rubbing it off with your finger or an eraser.

—*Jeniece Higgins, Northbrook, IL*

Page by Jeniece Higgins

Red-Hot Techniques

'I wish I was Peter Pan'
'I wish I could fly'
'I wish I was Captain Hook'
'Look at me Mum, I'm

magic

Life at four. Where the only troubles in the world are if there is icecream for dessert. Or a having skinned knee. Or not getting your own way every time. Your life is carefree and happy. Full of dreams about pirates and Peter Pan. Playing every minute of the day. Jumping on the trampoline. Laughing at your funny made up jokes. Life is one adventure after another. Being so loved by your family. Your childhood is a magical time, and that is how it should be.

SUNRISE til SUNSET

Page by Barbara Schipplock

Customize twill tape with rub-on words.

Supplies *Textured cardstock:* Bazzill Basics; *Patterned paper:* Daisy D's; *Letter stickers:* Sonnets, Creative Imaginations; *Eyelets:* Extreme Eyelets, Creative Imaginations; *Rub-ons:* Making Memories; *Computer font:* 2Peas Hot Chocolate, downloaded from *www.twopeasinabucket.com;* *Other:* Twill tape.

Easy Twill Tip

Here's an easy way to customize the popular look of printed twill tape. Choose a word from a sheet of rub-ons. Gently rub the letters onto your twill tape using the burnishing stick in the packaging, then carefully peel back the sheet.

—Barbara Schipplock
Manly West, QLD, Australia

technique

After aging your cardstock with walnut ink, scratch words into it for a worn, leathery look.

Supplies *Watercolor paper:* Strathmore; *Walnut ink:* Postmodern Design; *Eyelet letters and definition sticker:* Making Memories; *Buttons:* Luna Studios; *Buckle:* Diane's; *Cheesecloth:* Prym-Dritz; *Letter stamps:* PSX Design; *Stamping ink:* Ranger Industries; *Computer font:* My Type of Font, downloaded from the Internet; *Label:* me & my BIG ideas; *Linen canvas:* Pearl Paint; *Other:* Denim.

technique

Faux Leather Lettering

With three men in the house, I'm always looking for ways to add masculine flair to my pages. After a small accident involving a bowl of walnut ink, I discovered that I could "scratch" words into the page for a worn, leathery look. Just follow these steps:

❶ Select a heavyweight watercolor paper that won't buckle when wet. Write your words on the paper in pencil.

❷ Mix the walnut ink according to the package instructions. Liberally apply the walnut ink over your penciled words with a sponge brush. It's best to work in small sections.

❸ Using your penciled words as a guide, scratch the words into the paper. A paper-piercing tool or awl works great. The scratching should draw the walnut ink into the crevices. If you see white scratches, simply apply more walnut ink to that area.

❹ Let your page dry. The walnut ink will dry to a lighter shade of brown.

—Tracie Smith, Smithtown, NY

Walk with me Teach me

FATHER-HOOD
You are such a natural. The boys adore you. You teach them the right ways to go just by your own actions. I pray that they will continue to follow your direction and become great men. (Just like their dad!)

Westbury Gardens
May 2003

coach (kcch) 1. a trainer or instructor 2. one of significant experience and knowledge to mentor and teach regarding a specific activity.

HERO

Page by Tracie Smith

Try This Technique

by Lynne Montgomery

I first saw this pressed-velvet technique on a velvet pillow and was overjoyed to discover it works for scrapbooking, too! All you need is a scrap of velvet, a rubber stamp, a spray bottle and an iron. (When choosing a rubber stamp, keep in mind that more solid designs, as opposed to intricate designs with lots of lines, work better for this technique.)

To create this beautiful effect, lay the "right" side of the velvet over the rubber stamp. Lightly spray the back side with water, and with an iron set on low, iron over the back of the velvet. Remove the velvet from the stamp, and the impression of the stamp should be pressed into the velvet.

This elegant pressed-velvet look is a classy addition to a scrapbook page. *Pages by Lynne Montgomery.* **Supplies** *Patterned vellum:* Susan Branch, Colorbök; *Embossed paper:* Lasting Impressions for Paper; *Computer font:* CK Bella, "The Best of Creative Lettering" CD Vol. 4; *Rubber stamp:* American Art Stamp; *Circle punch:* Family Treasures; *Tag:* Avery Dennison; *Other:* Velvet, beads and fibers

Clearly Cool

*M*y son is enthralled with magic that's of the "now you see it, now you don't" variety. Although I suspect he just likes saying "ta da," he does enjoy making objects materialize and vanish before our very eyes (by quickly tossing them over his left shoulder).

I love using transparencies for the same reason—for their ability to appear and disappear. They can take center stage as embellished borders, frames or accents. They can also blend into the background, allowing other page elements to shine through.

Sturdy transparencies can take most anything you throw at them—computer printing, heat embossing, stamping, painting, writing, sanding, punching and tearing. And they're versatile. Use them for unobtrusive journaling blocks or for layered 3-D looks. Read on for more cool transparency techniques and tips. You'll find that these simple sheets can produce magical effects.

by
Denise Pauley

Transparencies: Magic Scraps

"Boys" by Loni Stevens, Pleasant Grove, UT. **Supplies** *Patterned paper:* K•I Memories; *Computer font:* Copperplate, Microsoft Word; *Paint:* Delta Technical Coatings; *Bookplate:* Li'l Davis Designs; *Eyelets:* Dritz; *Label:* me & my BIG ideas; *Letter stamps:* The Missing Link (Roman, upper and lower case) and Postmodern Design (Hodge Podge); *Other:* Date stamp, charm, safety pin, ribbon, staples and jump rings.

CREATE A "FLOATING FRAME"

Cut a transparency to the desired mat size, paint the edges with acrylic paint, then let the transparency dry before adhering a photo.

Helpful hint: Use spray adhesive directly behind the photo to attach the transparency. "You'll look like a master with a paint brush," says Loni, "since the lines are straight and no one can see the transparency!"

SWIPE IT!

Crystal-clear transparency sheets can be embellished on either side. To highlight journaling, apply acrylic paint, watercolors, rub-ons or chalk across the cardstock underneath the transparency.

You can also embellish the transparency to create a decorative photo mat. Just swipe it with acrylic paint, allow the paint to dry, then distress the painted sheet with fine sandpaper before adding ephemera.

Helpful hint: Attaching a transparency is a snap with brads, eyelets and other fasteners. A light coating of spray adhesive also does the trick. Or, affix the transparency with your favorite adhesive, then conceal the adhesive under another page element, such as a photo or accent block.

"Remotely Cute" by Denise Pauley, La Palma, CA. **Supplies** *Definition stickers, letter tiles, tag and brad:* Making Memories; *Transparency:* Stampendous!; *Typewriter key and elastic band:* 7 Gypsies; *Computer font:* Californian, Microsoft Word; *Alphabet stamps:* Ma Vinci's Reliquary; *Charms:* Westrim Crafts; *Paint:* Plaid Enterprises; *Chalk:* Craf-T Products.

"Blowing Bubbles" by Christine Brown, Hanover, MN. **Supplies** *Patterned papers:* Sonnets, Creative Imaginations and SEI; *Vellum:* It Takes Two; *Computer font:* 2Peas Chestnuts, downloaded from *www.twopeasinabucket.com*; *Transparency:* On a Roll, F & M Enterprises; *Pen:* American Crafts; *Alphabet charms:* Making Memories; *Stamping ink:* VersaMark, Tsukineko; *Embossing enamel:* Ultra Thick Embossing Enamel, Suze Weinberg; *Stamp n Bond,* Stampendous!; *Glitter:* Hampton Arts; *Eyelets:* Doodlebug Design.

GET "BUBBLY"

Use transparencies to simulate the look of bubbles for overlays, windows and accents. To create the look, follow these steps:

1. Cover a transparency with embossing ink.

2. Sprinkle embossing enamel on the wet ink, then heat.

3. While the enamel is still hot, sprinkle with Stamp n Bond and reheat. (Stamp n Bond is like embossing powder but becomes sticky when heated.)

4. Sprinkle a very light layer of crystal glitter over the sticky surface, then fully cover with another layer of embossing enamel and heat again.

5. Cut pieces for your windows from the finished iridescent transparency sheet.

Variations: Mix another color of embossing powder into the enamel for a tinted window. You can also sprinkle tiny sequins or mica flakes instead of glitter—experiment with different inclusions for a variety of glass effects.

PRINTING TIPS

When printing on transparencies, you have several options to prevent smearing. Keep these guidelines in mind:

- Most transparencies work with laser printers and copy machines. Check the packaging to determine archival quality.

- For ink-jet printers, purchase transparencies designed for your specific printer and select the "transparency" mode before printing. If the transparency is smooth and shiny on one side and a bit dull on the other, print on the dull side. *(Hint:* If you want the shiny side facing up, print a mirror image of your text on the dull side, then flip it over so the journaling can still be read.)

- If the transparency is not designated for an ink-jet printer, heat-set your text with clear embossing powder to help prevent smudging and add dimension.

Clearly Cool

CREATE "PAINTED" ACCENTS

Applying glass paint to transparencies affords you a multitude of translucent looks, including funky "painted" accents. Try the following:

- Apply a generous amount of glass paint to a transparency sheet. Depending on your desired texture, use a large brush, brayer or sponge to spread the paint.

- Ink a foam stamp (bold images work best) with embossing ink to prevent sticking, then carefully press into the wet paint. (The stamp will shimmy slightly.)

- For a "hand-painted" accent, apply various paints directly to the stamp, then press gently onto the transparency.

Helpful hint: Let your accent dry completely before loading your page into a protector.

Variations: Transparencies and glass paint can be used to create stained-glass accents, faux marbling, textured backgrounds, overlays and decorative pockets. *(Note:* If you're concerned about the archival safety of your paint, try this technique on cards or use duplicate photos.)

"Island Shopping" by Denise Pauley, La Palma, CA.
Supplies *Letter tiles, mini-eyelets and brad:* Making Memories; *Transparency:* Magic Scraps; *Stickers:* Creative Imaginations (postage stamps, postcards and letters) and Making Memories (definition); *Paint:* Plaid Enterprises; *Stamping ink:* Fresco, Stampa Rosa; *Pen:* Zig Millennium, EK Success; *Library pocket:* Anima Designs; *Charm:* Blue Moon; *Tags:* DMD, Inc. and Avery; *Other:* Foam stamp.

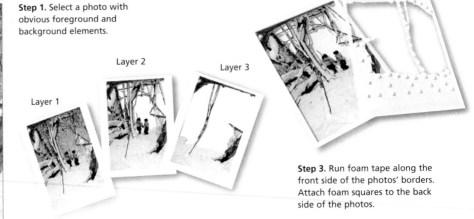

Step 1. Select a photo with obvious foreground and background elements.

Layer 1

Layer 2

Layer 3

Step 3. Run foam tape along the front side of the photos' borders. Attach foam squares to the back side of the photos.

Step 2. Cut layers from duplicate prints of the photo.

MAKE A SHADOW BOX

Love the look of shadow boxes? With transparencies, photo layers, foam tape and more, you can create a dimensional scene that looks like you're actually there. Here's how (see examples for steps 1-5).

1. **Select a photo.** Choose one with a lot of depth of field and obvious foreground and background elements. If your photo has prominent foreground, middle ground and background elements, you can use three copies of the photo to create a three-layer shadow box.

What if your photo only has a fore-ground and a background? You can still create a two-layer shadow box with two copies of the photo.

The photos will each need a ¼" border for mounting purposes. Ask your photo developer to print your photos with a white border. Or, if you output your own photos, leave a ¼" border around each when you trim it.

"Winter Wonderland" by Christine Brown, Hanover, MN. **Supplies** *Patterned paper:* Carolee's Creations; *Transparencies:* Hammermill; *Computer fonts:* FreshScript, downloaded from the Internet; 2Peas Hot Chocolate, downloaded from *www.twopeasinabucket.com*; *Stickers:* Jolee's Boutique, Sticko by EK Success; *Clear 3-D stickers:* Making Memories; *Adhesive tape:* Wonder Tape, Suze Weinberg; *Foam squares:* Therm O Web; *Fibers:* Rubba Dub Dub, Art Sanctum; On The Surface.

2. **Cut the photo layers.** Select one photo and cut away everything except those items that are closest to the camera. For Layer 1 (the top layer), Christine cut away everything but the tree, stump and snow closest to the camera.

For Layer 2 (the middle layer and that likely containing the most detail), cut away just the background elements.

Leave Layer 3 (the bottom layer) untouched. It will form your background.

3. **Prepare the layers.** Cut two pieces of transparency to the size of your photos (including the ¼" border). While the transparencies are optional, they add support and help create an "inside the box" feel. Adhere the transparencies to the back of the *top* two layers (Layers 1 and 2).

Run foam mounting tape around the entire border on the front side of the *bottom* two layers (Layers 2 and 3). Don't remove the protective covering yet.

Next, thoroughly cover the back side of the photos for Layers 1 and 2 with foam squares, leaving room along the outer edges where the mounting tape will be. Don't skimp! Be sure to put foam squares along all the edges inside the photo so they appear "lifted" in the finished shadow box. (*Hints:* Use foam squares or dots that are the same thickness as your border foam tape. You may need to cut some foam squares to fit behind the photos' smaller details.)

4. **Assemble the shadow box.** Working from the bottom up, remove the protective covering from the foam strips along the border of Layer 3 and from the foam squares on the back of Layer 2. Carefully align Layer 2 over Layer 3, then gently press down to create a strong bond between the layers. Repeat these steps with the top two layers. Your shadow box is complete!

5. **Incorporate the shadow box in your layout.** Measure the finished dimensions of your shadow box, then cut an opening of the same size in a piece of foam core. (You can save time with pre-scored foam core like that from Artistic Expressions.) If you need more height, use a double thickness of foam core.

Carefully fit the shadow box into the opening in the foam core, then cover the front and back seams with adhesive tape. You're ready to embellish your shadow box layout to your heart's content!

Step 4. Align layers to create a three-dimensional look.

Step 5. Fit the shadow box into a foam core frame.

Clearly Cool

OVERLAY A PHOTO

Design a layout with an altered-book feel. Print or photocopy a photo onto a transparency, then embellish it with stickers, rub-ons and ephemera as an overlay to a sheet of "text."

Helpful hint: Select an image with distinct light and dark tones. This helps the text show through yet allows your picture to be prominent.

"Beach Excursion" *by Faye Morrow Bell, Charlotte, NC.* **Supplies** *Patterned paper:* Design Originals; *Letter stickers:* Nostalgiques, EK Success; *Rubber stamp:* Stampers Anonymous; *Stamping ink:* Brilliance, Tsukineko; *Rub-ons:* Making Memories; *Pen:* Zig Writer, EK Success; *Punch:* The Punch Bunch; *Compass:* Collage Joy; *Ribbon:* C.M. Offray & Son; *Postage stamps and ticket stubs:* Limited Edition Rubber Stamps; *Other:* Transparency.

"Mr. and Mrs. Colorful Personality" *by Karen Burniston, Littleton, CO.* **Supplies** *Patterned papers:* Sonnets and Teri Martin, Creative Imaginations; *Transparency:* Inkjet Transparencies, Epson; *Computer font:* SF Wonder Comic, downloaded from the Internet; *Letter stickers:* Sonnets, Creative Imaginations; *Date stamp, clear 3-D stickers and eyelets:* Making Memories; *Rub-ons:* Bradwear ("Colorful"), Alphawear ("Karl" and "Emma") and Tagwear (on round tag), Creative Imaginations.

CHANGE YOUR IMAGE

Can't decide between a black-and-white or color photo? Use both! A photo printed on a transparency sheet is part of this interactive page technique, which allows the image to instantly change. To create the effect, follow these steps:

1. Open a color photo (scanned or digital) in photo-editing software and save a copy. Print the color photo on premium photo paper. *(Hint:* Increase the saturation levels so the photo is rich with color. The transparency overlay will dull the colors considerably.)

2. Open the saved copy of the photo and convert it to black and white. Print it on a transparency designed for your printer type.

3. Align the transparency photo exactly over the color photo. Adhere the photos along the left and right sides. Leave the top and bottom edges open.

4. Trim a piece of patterned paper to the width of the photos and slide it between the photos from the top edge. The photo will appear black and white with a patterned paper background.

Looking for transparencies? Try these creative and artistic offerings:

"Abundance"
by Martha Crowther, Salem, NH

Supplies *Transparency:* Clearly Creative, Magic Scraps; *Leaf charm and frame:* All the Extras; *Fibers:* Fibers by the Yard; *Key:* Li'l Davis Designs; *Ruler:* Nostalgiques, EK Success; *Rub-ons:* Simply Stated, Making Memories.

• **Magic Scraps** (*www.magicscraps.com*)

"Le Memoire of a Little Man"
by Lilac Chang, San Mateo, CA

Supplies *Transparencies:* Narratives, Creative Imaginations; *Patterned papers:* Sharon Soneff, Creative Imaginations; Legacy Collage (script), Design Originals; *Brads:* Lost Art Treasures; *Textured paper:* Jonah Sutherland Collection, Far and Away; *Rub-ons and 3-D letter stickers:* Making Memories; *Typewriter keys:* EK Success; *Letter stamps:* PSX Design; *Stamping ink:* StazOn, Ranger Industries; *Computer font:* Garamouche, P22 Type Foundry; *Other:* Ribbon

• **Creative Imaginations**
(*www.cigift.com*)

Magic with Mica

PHOTO © ERIC SCHRAMM

by Dawn Brookey

I remember the first time I saw mica at a rubber stamp store. The product was unusual and interesting, and I couldn't wait to experiment with it.

After purchasing the entire stock (I told you I was intrigued), I drove straight home to play with it. Before long, I discovered that I could do almost anything with this versatile, acid-free product. Here are some of my favorite techniques. Need a little help getting started? See "Mica Basics" on page 121.

Creative uses for mica

fashionable frames

Mica tiles make fabulous photo frames. Layer tiles over a photo to accentuate an image. Or, create a frame by following these steps:

❶ Cut your mica into four strips.

❷ Stamp or emboss the strips with words or images.

❸ Punch holes in the strips, then connect them with jump rings.

❹ Embellish the frame with wire clips or other embellishments.

Frame by Dawn Brookey. **Supplies** *Patterned paper:* Rusty Pickle; *Mica:* USArtQuest; *Jump rings:* Westrim Crafts; *Rubber stamp:* PSX Design; *Stamping ink:* StazOn, Tsukineko; *Other:* Heart clip.

torn tiles

A thin sheet of mica is easy to tear. For the embellishment on this layout, here's what to do:

❶ Tear layers of mica to follow the shape of the stamped image. (If necessary, you can start the tear by cutting a small slit.)

❷ Peel the mica to create two separate pieces.

❸ Sandwich a stamped image between the mica layers, then fan the elements so each is exposed.

Page by Dawn Brookey. **Supplies** *Mica:* USArtQuest; *Computer font:* 2Peas Evergreen, downloaded from *www.twopeasinabucket.com; Radiant pearls:* Angelwing Enterprises; *Letter stamps:* Hero Arts; *Date stamp:* Costco; *Handmade paper:* Artistic Scrapper, Creative Imaginations; *Stamping ink:* VersaMark, Tsukineko; Memories (black), Stewart Superior Corporation; ColorBox (copper), Clearsnap; *Embossing enamel:* Suze Weinberg; *Embossing powder:* Stamp Mania (platinum) and Stamp-n-Stuff (copper); *Metal frame:* Scrapworks; *Fibers:* Rubba Dub Dub, Art Sanctum; On The Surface; Artistic Enhancements; *Other:* Photo mat and leaf stamp.

Mica Basics

Mica is a lustrous, rock-forming mineral. Artists love to use its layers to create stunning artistic effects. Here's how to separate and adhere mica.

Separating Mica

Vary the color intensity of your mica by separating its many layers. Here's how:

1. Carefully push your thumbnail into the edge of the mica tile until the layer (or layers) starts to separate.

2. Gently peel back the layer (or layers). This will be similar to peeling back a page from a magnetic album sheet.

3. The thinner the mica, the more flexible it is. For a watery look, peel the mica as thin as possible so the amber tint can no longer be detected.

Adhering Mica

Mica is translucent, so you'll need to be creative to hide any adhesive. Here are three recommendations:

- Hide glue dots or adhesive tabs under embellishments.
- Experiment with brads, eyelets, snaps, staples, safety pins and conchos for more dimensional effects (see sample).
- Adhere mica with products such as Diamond Glaze, Crystal Lacquer or Perfect Paper Adhesive. Krylon spray adhesive is acid-free and works great, too!

Sample by Dawn Brookey. **Supplies** *Patterned paper:* Li'l Davis Designs; *Mica and adhesive:* USArtQuest; *Stamping ink:* Marvy Uchida; *Concho:* Scrapworks; *Clear 3-D word sticker:* Sonnets, Creative Imaginations; *Other:* Ribbon.

collage creations

Mica adds depth and a vintage touch to any image placed behind it. Take advantage of the product's form by pressing patterned paper, photos and other accents between layers. To create the look of the "Promise" tag shown here:

❶ Separate a mica tile into three pieces.

❷ Lightly coat the bottom sheet with Perfect Paper Adhesive. Place a small swatch of patterned paper on top.

❸ Layer the second piece of mica over the first sheet. Apply another coat of adhesive, then adhere mesh and an image.

❹ Adhere the top mica layer. Stamp a collage image with solvent ink, then add charms.

Variations: Try encasing images inside two pieces of mica. You can also collage your photos. For another great idea, see Lilac Chang's photo collage of her son in her layout on page 123.

Sample by Dawn Brookey. **Supplies** *Patterned paper, mica, mica flakes and adhesive:* USArtQuest; *Rubber stamp:* The Moon Rose; *Stamping ink:* StazOn, Tsukineko; *Image:* ARTchix Studio; *Other:* Mesh and charms.

change the color

Changing your mica color is a snap with these three simple steps:

❶ Separate the layers.

❷ Rub or drop ink or paint between the layers. You can add inclusions, such as mica flakes, glitter, flower petals, pigment powders and more.

❸ Reposition the layers. For this example, I used blue dye-reinker drops and mica flakes.

Sample by Dawn Brookey. **Supplies** *Mica, mica flakes and adhesive:* USArtQuest; *Rubber stamp:* River City Rubber Works; *Stamping ink:* StazOn, Tsukineko; Marvy Uchida; *Other:* Craft wire and mesh.

Page by Lilac Chang. **Supplies** *Paper:* K & Company; *Mica:* USArtQuest; *Stencil:* Headline Sign; *Brads:* Lost Art Treasures; *Page pebble:* Making Memories; *Sticker:* EK Success; *Computer font:* Garamouche, P22 Type Foundry.

stamp stuff

Mica is ideal for stamping and embossing because it's heat resistant. The tiles have a glass-like surface, which means you'll need to use permanent ink (or heat-emboss your image) to prevent smearing. I like to stamp identical images on multiple layers to create depth. To achieve the look shown here:

❶ Choose two mica tiles of similar shape or split one tile into two pieces.

❷ Stamp a background image on cardstock.

❸ Stamp and emboss images in gold on one tile.

❹ Stamp images in black solvent ink on the other tile. Layer the pieces so the patterns show through the mica.

Variation: Brush acrylic paint on a tile. After the paint dries, stamp your image with solvent ink.

Sample by Dawn Brookey. **Supplies** *Mica:* USArtQuest; *Rubber stamps:* Stampin' Up! and Club Scrap; *Stamping ink:* StazOn and Brilliance, Tsukineko; ColorBox, Clearsnap; *Embossing powder:* Stampendous!

Page by Dawn Brookey. **Supplies** *Patterned paper:* Li'l Davis Designs (sewing pattern); 7 Gypsies (tape measure); Rusty Pickle (woman); *Mica:* Coffee Break Design; *Computer fonts:* Carpenter ITC and American Typewriter, downloaded from the Internet; *Rubber stamps:* Dawn Houser (dress) and Hero Arts (date); *Stamping ink:* StazOn, Tsukineko (black); ColorBox (gold), Clearsnap; *Embossing enamel:* Suze Weinberg; *Word pebble and oval frame:* Li'l Davis Designs; *Metal frame:* Making Memories; *Buckle:* La Mode; *Other:* Brads, gold tag and filigree.

Idea to note: Dawn embossed her frame with gold stamping ink and embossing enamel.

Page by Dawn Brookey.
Supplies *Patterned papers:*
Chatterbox (stripes and
blue); Making Memories
(floral); 7 Gypsies (measur-
ing tape); Sonnets (script),
Creative Imaginations;
Mica and dried flower:
USArtQuest; *Diamond
glaze:* JudiKins; *Computer
font:* Cochin, downloaded
from the Internet; *Rubber
stamps:* Stampland (por-
trait) and Anna Griffin (corner); *Stamping ink:* StazOn,
Tsukineko; *Metal words,
definition, clear 3-D sticker
and circle clip:* Making
Memories; *Clock accent:*
Uponacharm.com; *Jump
rings:* Westrim Crafts; *Paint:*
Ceramcoat, Delta Technical
Coatings; *Chalk:* Craft-T
Products; *Other:* Washers,
craft wire and brads.

Idea to note: Dawn coated
her dried flower with a
glaze.

mini mica book

Use large mica tiles of varying sizes and shapes
to create a layered mini-book. Follow these steps:
❶ Choose three tiles of similar size and opacity.
If necessary, trim one side to make binding easier.
❷ Stamp the top tile with a large image.
❸ Carefully separate the second tile into two
pieces.
❹ Trim two photos and place them back-to-back.
Adhere the photos together. Place them between
the separate layers of the second tile. Line them
up with the left side so they'll be bound.
❺ Press the layers together, then secure them
with brads.
❻ Print your journaling on patterned paper.
Adhere the journaling pages back to back. Using
the third tile, repeat steps 3, 4 and 5.
❼ Place another photo behind the last page.
❽ Punch holes in the tiles and bind with jump
rings.
❾ Secure the book to your layout using craft
wire and small washers. ♥

Mica Manufacturers

You can purchase mica from the following suppliers:

USArtQuest
www.usartquest.com
Phone: 517/522-6225
MSRP: $5.76-$19.99

Coffee Break Design
Phone: 317/290-1542
MSRP: $8-$16

STENCIL IT!

Create cool letter and number looks

by
Dawn Brookey

WHEN I WAS A TEENAGER (and before computers became mainstream), I made school posters with big cardboard stencils and spray paint. Remember those? My school was littered with stenciled signs for car washes, band concerts and student body elections.

Well, stencil lettering is back. As one of today's hottest trends, you'll find it everywhere—on crosswalks, on curbs, on billboards, on military uniforms and more. Why, I've even seen stencil lettering on storm drain covers!

While the stencils of the past were mere lettering tools, the stencils of today are so much more. They're inexpensive, versatile and perfect for scrapbook pages. You can use them often and never tire of the results. Here are some new techniques to try on your next project.

Creative Ways to **ALTER** Your Stencils

While packaged cardboard stencils may appear a bit drab, you can turn them into fabulous page accents with a few simple techniques.

Layer it.

Give your letters instant color and texture by placing a stencil over materials like ribbon or embossed paper. Following are two cool examples by Angie Cramer and Renee Camacho.

Interested in a few variations? Try this technique with fibers, faux fur, patterned paper, fabrics, metal, mesh or beads.

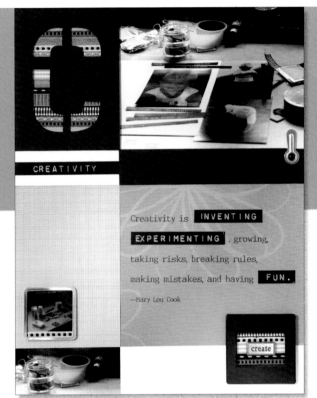

Create a riveting look by placing your letter on a ribbon background.

Page by Angie Cramer. **Supplies** *Ribbon, metal-rimmed tag and metal word:* Making Memories; *Computer font for "C":* Incognito, downloaded from the Internet; *Photo anchor:* 7 Gypsies; *Label:* Dymo; *Other:* Slide holder.

Add visual interest by stitching the stencil over embossed paper.

Page by Renee Camacho. **Supplies** *Handmade paper:* Jennifer Collection; *"C":* Creative Imaginations; *Brads:* Lost Art Treasures; *"Cherish" rubber stamp:* Rubber Moon; *Walnut ink:* 7 Gypsies; *Additional "Cs":* Index card, stencil and label from label maker.

Paint stencils to coordinate with the colors on the layout.

Page by Dawn Brookey. **Supplies** *Stencils for "P" and "W":* Headline Sign; *Metal stencil letters for "BALL":* Li'l Davis Designs; *Acrylic paint:* Delta Technical Coatings; *Rubber stamps:* Green Pepper Press (alphabet) and JudiKins (diamond); *Metal mesh:* Making Memories; *Label:* Dymo; *Stamping ink:* StazOn, Tsukineko; *Other:* Encyclopedia pages.

2 Paint it.

Want to change the stencil's color or give the item a weathered appearance? Try acrylic paint!

Sand metal stencils before painting them to help paint adhere to the surface.

For an imperfect image, apply paint unevenly to your rubber stamp and use textured cardstock.

Create an antiqued appearance by brushing acrylic paint directly on your stencil, then sanding it to expose the cardboard below.

Supplies *Stencil:* Headline Sign; *Acrylic paint:* Delta Technical Coatings.

Apply a thick base coat of crackle medium under white paint to produce this distressed look.

Supplies *Stencil:* Headline Sign; *Crackle medium:* Plaid Folk Art; *Acrylic paint:* Delta Technical Coatings; *Patterned paper:* Mustard Moon; *Photo flip:* Making Memories; *Photo dart:* 7 Gypsies; *Brad:* creativeimpressions.com.

All letter examples by Dawn Brookey.

3 Cover it.

Embellish the stencil with beads, sequins, tinsel, sand or glitter. To create a watery look like that in this layout:

1. Brush the stencil with white acrylic paint and let it dry.

2. Apply spray adhesive to the stencil, then sprinkle beads over the whole surface.

3. Shake off any excess beads and adhere the stencil to a black tag.

4. To make the blue background paper, pour two shades of blue and white paint side by side on a paper plate. Dip a paintbrush into the paint so all three colors are on the brush. Using long strokes, brush the paint across your page in one direction.

5. Paint the washers with white paint so the color goes into the crevices. Wipe the surface of the washer with a damp towel to remove the excess paint.

6. Create a custom title by using letters from different rub-on words.

Embellish your stencil with beads or other fun materials.

Page by Dawn Brookey. **Supplies** *Stencil:* Headline Sign; *Acrylic paint:* Delta Technical Coatings; *Washer words, ribbon, metal frame and rub-on letters (taken from different words):* Making Memories; *Spray adhesive:* Krylon; *Label:* Dymo; *Brads:* creativeimpressions.com; *Other:* Paint chip and glass beads.

Where to Find Stencil Products

Stencil products can be found in virtually any craft, office, or home improvement store. They range from simple cardboard varieties to embellishments made specifically for paper crafts. Look for products from the following manufacturers:

- Autumn Leaves
- Creative Imaginations
- EK Success
- Fusion Art Stamps
- Headline Sign

- Li'l Davis Designs
- Ma Vinci's Reliquary
- Scrapworks
- Stampers Anonymous
- The C-Thru Ruler Co.

Other STENCIL LOOKS by Dawn

Dress up your stencils with the following techniques, then add the letters and numbers to your pages.

Create a glass finish by inking a stencil and embossing it with clear embossing powder.

Supplies *Stencil:* Headline Sign; *Stamping ink:* ColorBox, Clearsnap; *Embossing powder:* JudiKins; *Modeling paste:* Liquitex; *Brads and metal mesh:* Making Memories.

Add an antiqued look with a crackle finish.

Supplies *Stencil:* Headline Sign; *Embossing stamping ink:* Boss Gloss; *Embossing powder:* JudiKins; *Stamping ink:* Memories, Stewart Superior Corporation.

To create a unique crackle finish:

1. Emboss your stencil with embossing ink and silver powder.

2. Once it's cool, bend the stencil to create cracks.

3. Rub a black inkpad directly over the stencil.

4. Wipe the stencil surface with a clean cloth to remove excess ink. The ink will settle in the cracks and accentuate the look.

Dab purple ink directly onto your stencil.

Supplies *Stencil:* Headline Sign; *Stamping ink:* Ink It; *Metal corners:* Making Memories.

Get the look of aged metal by embossing the stencil with different metallic powders, then sanding it.

Supplies *Stencil:* Headline Sign; *Embossing stamping ink:* Boss Gloss; *Silver, gold and copper embossing powders:* JudiKins.

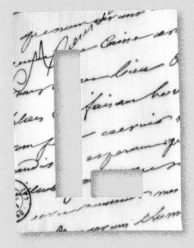

Stamp an image over a painted stencil, then coat it with glaze.

Supplies *Stencil:* Headline Sign; *Acrylic paint:* Delta Technical Coatings; *Rubber stamp:* Hero Arts; *Stamping ink:* StazOn, Tsukineko; *Glaze:* Ranger Industries.

Using Your Stencils as **TOOLS**

If you're like me, it's easy to forget that stencils are traditionally used to create letters. Once you get past the urge to alter the stencils, you can use them as tools to invent cool letters or numbers on virtually any surface. Here's how.

Painting

Painting with stencils is easy and highly addictive. Acrylic paints are the easiest to use and can be found in virtually any color.

Paint letters onto a transparency for an eye-catching title.

Page by Dawn Brookey. **Supplies** *Stencil:* Headline Sign; *Transparency:* 3M; *Acrylic paint:* Delta Technical Coatings; *Rubber stamps:* Fusion Art Stamps ("enjoy"), Hero Arts (journaling) and Plaid Enterprises (design); *Stamping ink:* StazOn, Tsukineko; *Patterned paper and woven label:* me & my BIG ideas; *Leaf sticker:* Pebbles Inc.; *Metal frame and tags:* Making Memories; *Label:* Dymo; *Buttons:* Junkitz.

Let each letter dry before stenciling the next one. After all the letters were painted, Dawn masked off squares with sticky notes and dabbed on paint to create the straight lines.

Experiment with paint on a variety of fabric surfaces.

Supplies *Stencil:* Headline Sign; *Acrylic paint:* Delta Technical Coatings; *Fabric:* K & Company; *Ribbon:* Li'l Davis Designs; *Brads:* creativeimpressions.com.

Construct a dynamic title with stencil stickers.

Supplies *Stencil stickers:* Nostalgiques by EK Success; *Acrylic paint:* Delta Technical Coatings; *Acrylic gesso:* Liquitex; *Tin sheet:* Artistic Expressions; *Patterned papers:* Creative Imaginations (green) and Daisy D's (pink floral); *Rubber stamps:* Hero Arts (alpha) and Making Memories (date); *Stamping ink:* StazOn, Tsukineko; *Silk ribbon:* Memory Lane; *Computer font:* Garamouche, P22 Type Foundry.

Dawn softened the patterned paper with pink paint before printing the title.

Three Stencil Tips

Consider the following when working with stencils:

• *Use a brush with a flat surface.* I prefer sponge spouncers because they're inexpensive and their small surfaces are perfect for even the most petite stencils. You can also use larger stencil brushes, make-up sponges, sponge daubers, or an ordinary foam brush. They're all available at craft and hardware stores.

• *Test your tape.* When using tape to adhere a stencil, test a small area on your paper first to make sure it won't tear when the tape is removed. To remove some of the tape adhesive, press it to your clothing or hand several times before applying it to your paper. Sticky notes and temporary adhesive dots can also be used to adhere stencils to delicate papers.

• *Cover surrounding areas.* When stenciling directly onto a layout, mask off the area around the stencil with sticky notes and paper to avoid accidental splatter.

Ideas to note: To create this look, Dawn adhered the "O" sticker to a title block and dabbed the inside of the letter with brown paint. She carefully lifted the sticker to expose the letter. She then painted the edges of the "J" and "Y" stickers and adhered them to the title block.

How to Stencil

Follow these steps to create beautiful stenciled letters in a flash.

1. Position the stencil and secure it in place with low-tack tape or temporary adhesive.

2. Pour a small amount of acrylic paint onto a paper plate.

3. Lightly dip the end of a stencil brush into the paint, blotting the brush lightly on the edge of the plate to remove the excess. Do not overload the brush with paint or it will seep under the edge of the stencil.

4. Holding the brush straight up and down, lightly dab paint onto the stencil opening. Continue dabbing the paint until the entire area is covered.

5. Carefully lift the stencil to reveal your painted image. The stencil can be reused once dry.

Stencil Variations WITH PAINT

Once you've got the basics down, try these additional looks:

• Use two colors of acrylic paint on the stencil for a shadow effect.

• Add texture by applying paint with a sea sponge, rag or plastic wrap.

• Mix paint and glaze for a transparent look.

• Spray over your stencil with spray paint.

Accent by Dawn Brookey. **Supplies** *Stencil:* Headline Sign; *Spray paint:* Krylon.

To create this look, adhere a paper stencil to cardboard with temporary adhesive. Holding the spray paint can about 8" away, spray over the stencil with short spurts. To avoid overspraying around the stencil itself, mask off the surrounding area with paper or sticky notes.

Accents by Renee Camacho. **Supplies** *Stencil and patterned paper:* Autumn Leaves; *Computer font:* Highlight, Autumn Leaves; *Acrylic paint:* Delta Technical Coatings; *Button:* Making Memories; *Brads:* Lost Art Treasures.

To create a stippled letter look (left), adhere your stencil to a piece of paper. Take a piece of wadded-up plastic and apply acrylic paint in a dabbing motion, twisting your hand continually to vary the shading and look. Remove the stencil. Once the paint is dry, embellish the letter as desired.

Working with an extra-cool stencil? Include it as part of your design (right) and attach a printed title, journaling and embellishments. Note how Renee placed patterned paper behind the stencil and stitched around the letter.

Stencil Variations WITHOUT PAINT

Step it up by creating other exciting looks with stamping ink, embossing powders and modeling paste.

Supplies *Stencil:* Headline Sign; *Stamping ink:* ColorBox, Clearsnap; *Embossing powder:* Amazing Glaze, JudiKins; *Map:* me & my BIG ideas; *Brads:* Making Memories; *Other:* Circle tags, jump ring and charm.

To create this look, position your stencil over the rough side of shrink plastic. Dab ink in an up-and-down motion over the stencil's letter opening. Carefully lift the stencil, punch holes, then shrink plastic according to the package directions.

Note: You will need to use a large stencil (3" or larger) since the image will shrink significantly. Also, it's easier to work with small inkpads such as the ColorBox Cat's Eye variety or removable triangles.

Supplies *Stencil:* The C-Thru Ruler Co.; *Stamping ink:* ColorBox, Clearsnap; *Shrink plastic:* Shrinky Dinks; *Label:* Dymo; *Patterned paper:* KI Memories; *Other:* Beads and wire.

Supplies *Stencil:* Headline Sign; *Modeling paste:* Liquitex; *Patterned paper, ribbon and ribbon charm:* Making Memories.

Dry Embossing

Push your stencils to the limit by using them to dry-emboss letters and numbers on different surfaces. To emboss metal for an edgy look:

1. Place a metal sheet on a soft surface, such as a mousepad or cardboard.

2. Position your stencil backward over the metal sheet.

3. Using an embossing stylus, trace the shape of the letter.

4. Lift the stencil and turn the metal sheet face up.

5. Lightly swipe sandpaper over the surface of your embossed letter to roughen the image. Rub an ink pad across the letter and wipe away the excess.

Take your stencils for a dry-embossing spin. *Page by Dawn Brookey.*

Supplies *Stencil:* Headline Sign; *Patterned paper and metal stencil:* Li'l Davis Designs; *Metal sheet:* Making Memories; *Brads:* creativeimpressions.com.

Create a shabby-chic look on patterned paper by sanding the embossed image to expose the paper's white center. *Tag by Dawn Brookey.*

Supplies *Stencil:* Headline Sign, *Patterned papers:* Magenta (dark blue) and me & my BIG ideas (light blue); *Ribbon and brad:* Making Memories; *Label:* Dymo; *Safety pin:* Li'l Davis Designs; *Rubber stamps:* PSX Design; *Stamping ink:* Memories, Stewart Superior Corporation; *Other:* Jewelry tags.

"Engrave" your letter on a transparency to create a cool etched look. *Accent by Dawn Brookey.*

Supplies *Stencil:* Headline Sign; *Printed transparency and engraving tool:* Magic Scraps; *Stitching template:* Li'l Davis Designs; *Other:* String.

Duplicate the embossed look on a printed transparency with an engraving tool. Here's how:

1. With low-tack tape, adhere the stencil backward on the rough side of a printed transparency.

2. Use an engraving tool to trace along the shape of the letter.

3. Turn the transparency over so its smooth side is facing upward. Embellish.

3 Cutting Out Letters

You can make stencil letters and numbers out of paper, cardstock or even clay! Simply position the stencil backward on the reverse side of the paper, trace the letter with a pencil, and cut it out using sharp scissors or an X-acto knife.

Create a clever clay number. *Example by Dawn Brookey.*

Supplies *Stencil:* Headline Sign; *Clay:* Premo, Sculpey.

To create colorful clay stencil accents:

1. Knead together pearl and gold clay to create a marbled color.

2. Flatten clay with a rolling pin or pasta machine.

3. Position a stencil over the clay and cut out a number with an X-acto knife.

4. Lift the stencil and remove the number pieces.

5. Bake the clay according to its package directions.

Add instant color by cutting your stencil numbers from striped paper and placing them on the layout. *Page by Lee Anne Russell.*

Supplies *Patterned paper:* KI Memories; *Letter stamps and stencils:* Ma Vinci; *Letter buttons:* Junkitz; *Embossing powder:* Opals; *Stamping ink:* Stampin' Up!; *Computer fonts:* 2Peas My Muse, downloaded from www.twopeasinabucket.com; American Typewriter, downloaded from the Internet; *Brads:* American Tag; *Other:* Twine and metal embellishments.

Cut out the number and use your new stencil on your project. Place pink paper behind the cut-out area to add color. *Tag by Dawn Brookey.*

Supplies *Stencil:* Headline Sign; *Patterned paper and circle tag:* KI Memories; *Label:* Dymo; *Metal frame:* Li'l Davis Designs; *Ribbon:* Making Memories; *Stamping ink:* Memories, Stewart Superior Corporation; *Brads:* creativeimpressions.com; *Other:* Metal-rimmed tag

Add texture to clay by pressing in a rubber stamp before baking. *Example by Dawn Brookey.*

Supplies *Stencil:* Headline Sign; *Clay:* Premo, Sculpey; *Rubber stamp:* Toy Box.

Getting the Stencil LOOK without a Stencil

Don't have stencils? You can get the stencil look with computer fonts and rubber stamps.

SCRAPBOOKER LONI STEVENS recently came up with two terrific ideas while visiting a craft boutique. "While there, I saw framed pictures where the inside mat had the cut-out phrase 'Boys Will Be Boys,' " says Loni. "Behind each letter was a photograph. I knew I wanted to use this cool technique in my scrapbooking." Her example appears below.

Supplies *Screws:* Making Memories; *Beaded chain:* Li'l Davis Designs; *Metal hardware:* 7 Gypsies; *Adhesive-backed metal paper:* Magic Scraps; *Computer fonts:* Andale Mono, Steamer and Trendy University, downloaded from the Internet.

To create a "Quarterback" example like this:

1. Choose a stencil font (you can download a version online).

2. Click on the WordArt feature in Microsoft Word. Type in and manipulate your letter or number. (Loni chose "8" to represent the number on her brother's football jersey.)

3. Change the shading by selecting Format from the Format menu. Under Format, select Borders & Shading. Click on the Shading tab for options to fill the text background with black ink. Change the fill color to white to leave the background blank for your patterns.

4. Change your printer's media type to "Photo Quality Glossy Film" for the best output quality. *Note:* Loni tried the "Ink Jet Transparency" option, but noticed that it left fine lines.

5. After outputting the image to your transparency, let it dry, then handle the transparency with gloves to avoid transferring fingerprints.

Loni wanted her accent to be a "badge" that pays tribute to her brother and his team. She placed the entire picture behind a transparency. Loni selected white ink as the fill for her subtitles so they'd be clear, then placed strips of white and red cardstock behind the words.

FOR A FUN VARIATION, place patterned paper rather than photographs behind your letter. Loni chose a coordinating set of paper and embellishments so everything would match perfectly. Note how versatile her accent is. "It includes a perforated crease," says Loni, "so you can use the accent as a journaling block when closed. Or, lift the tab to open the accent and see hidden journaling inside. I adhered a tiny piece of Velcro inside to keep my accent closed most of the time."

Supplies *Transparency:* Hammermill; *Patterned paper and tab:* KI Memories; *Flower, ribbon and brad:* Making Memories; *Computer fonts:* Prestige Elite, Adobe and Billie Kid, downloaded from the Internet.

Where to Find Stencil Fonts

You can download free stencil fonts from a number of online sites. Visit *www.fontseek.com* for help finding them. Go to *www.twopeasinabucket.com*, and you can download (for a small fee) two new stencil fonts by Jennifer McGuire. Free Mac/PC downloads are available from *www.dafont.com*.

New fonts by Jennifer McGuire:

2Peas Frazzled Stencil
2 Peas Frazzled Stencil

2 Peas Frazzled Stencil Negative

Sample fonts from www.dafont.com:

DEPRESSIONIST THREE
Depressionist Three

WELTRON URBAN
Weltron Urban

TRENDY UNIVERSITY
Trendy University

TINSNIPS
Tinsnips

Stencilia Bold
Stencilia Bold

PRODUCT
Product

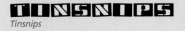
Malermeister

Add the stencil look to your pages quickly and easily with rubber stamps. *Page by Dawn Brookey.*

Supplies *Stencil for "B":* Headline Sign; *Rubber stamps:* Fusion Art Stamps; *Brads:* Making Memories; *Acrylic paint:* Delta Technical Coatings; *Stamping ink:* Memories, Stewart Superior Corporation; *Patterned paper:* Autumn Leaves (nautical) and me & my BIG ideas (diamond); *Other:* Fabric. *Idea to note:* Dawn stenciled the letter B on the fabric with acrylic paint.

Stamp directly onto packing tape for a wet look. *Accent by Dawn Brookey.*

Supplies *Rubber stamps:* Ma Vinci's Reliquary; *Stamping ink:* StazOn, Tsukineko; *Patterned paper:* Making Memories (blue) and SEI (diamond); *Beach image:* Pebbles Inc.; *Brads:* Making Memories; *Acrylic paint:* Delta Technical Coatings; *Other:* Canvas, jump ring, charm, packing tape and ribbon.

Next time you're searching for a dynamic page accent, reach for a stencil. Experiment with some of these techniques and invent a few of your own. Whether you use stencils as embellishments or lettering tools, you'll be delighted with the results.

More STENCIL LOOKS by Dawn

Getting hooked on stenciling? Here are more looks to try to add a cool creative touch.

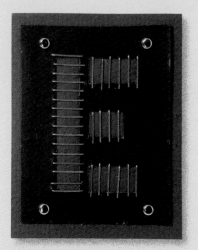

Dab black ink onto a stencil, then staple along the shape of the letter.

Supplies *Stencil:* Headline Sign; *Brads:* Making Memories; *Stamping ink:* Memories, Stewart Superior Corporation; *Other:* Staples.

Add a terrific touch with tinted modeling paste.

Supplies *Stencil:* Headline Sign; *Modeling paste:* Liquitex; *Acrylic paint:* Delta Technical Coatings.

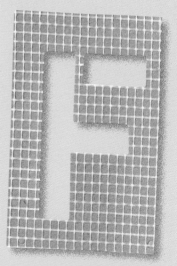

Cover your stencil with adhesive mesh.

Supplies *Stencil:* Headline Sign; *Other:* Mesh.

To create two cool accents by covering a stencil with tinted modeling paste:

1. Tint modeling paste by mixing in a few drops of red and blue acrylic paint.

2. Adhere your stencil to a piece of wax paper.

3. Using a palette knife, spread white modeling paste across the middle third of the stencil surface. Be sure to fill in the letter space.

4. Spread blue and red tinted paste across the top and bottom thirds of the stencil. Let the paste dry.

5. Carefully lift the stencil from the wax paper. You'll see a colorful image of the number on wax paper—and your stencil will be decorated beautifully.

Crumple your stencil and ink it for added dimension.

Supplies *Stencil:* Headline Sign; *Stamping ink:* Rubber Stampede.

Decoupage your stencil with patterned tissue and stickers.

Supplies *Stencil:* Headline Sign; *Decoupage paste:* Plaid Enterprises; *Printed tissue and transparency:* 7 Gypsies; *Clear stickers:* NRN Designs.

terrific
Text
six totally tactile

I'm not accident prone—unless I'm scrapbooking! Aside from a few scrap-related injuries, most of my accidents have been on actual pages. I'm willing to wager I've ruined more cardstock than layouts I've completed. Still, many of my mishaps have turned into **happy accidents!**

Such is the case with **texture transfer.** The first time I tried dry embossing, I definitely lacked know-how. After finishing my project, I lifted it up and found that not only had I made a poor impression, I'd picked up an annoying texture

by Darcee Thompson

...ture

techniques

from my table. (I thought you had to rub the entire area very thoroughly with a tool to raise the image.) I was disappointed that I didn't get the expected results. Happily, though, my "mistake" led to an **exciting discovery:** I could transfer any texture onto cardstock!

With this discovery, I started noticing textures on ceilings, floor mats, wood, toys and more. I now transfer them directly onto my scrapbook pages. Transferring texture has become one of my **favorite scrapbooking techniques.**

Let's go over the basics and what you need to get started. See facing page for results.

step 1

Texture. This can come from a template or around the house. (Make sure your texture is clean and secure.)

step 2

Waxed paper. This creates a lubricant to help the embossing tool glide over the paper.

step 3

Tape. I use low-tack *and* sticky tapes. I apply low-tack tape directly to my cardstock, then overlap it with sticky tape onto the texture. This secures the cardstock to the texture and lets me easily remove the tape without tearing my cardstock.

step 4

Embossing tool. The trick to transferring texture is to hold your tool perpendicular to your paper. The Empressor by Chatterbox lets me work fast because it's bigger and won't tear my paper. It won't create deep impressions, so I use a stylus to transfer more distinct and deep textures. Because this tool is smaller, the paper tears more easily. I usually use a combination of both tools.

Page by Darcee Thompson. **Supplies** *Texture template:* Carolee's Creations; *Transparency:* Pockets on a Roll, F & M Enterprises; *Stamping ink:* Fresca, Stampa Rosa; *Leafing pen:* Krylon; *Mini brads:* Making Memories; *Embossing powder:* Stampendous!; *Embossing enamel:* Suze Weinberg; *Embossing tool:* Hot Boss, Carolee's Creations; *Computer font:* CK Evolution, "Fresh Fonts" CD, *Creating Keepsakes*.

Texture Enhancements

Once you've transferred your texture, you can enhance it in a variety of ways. Experiment with any combination from the following list:

- Chalk
- Metallic rub-ons
- Colored pencils
- Pigment powders
- Stamping ink
- Lacquer
- Sanding

Over time, I've discovered a few ways to vary the basic look. Try your hand at some of the following texture transfer techniques, and let your scrapbook pages make a great impression!

Wet Transfer

Get your cardstock wet for this option—it'll make the rubbing less tedious and produce more attractive results. You can transfer deeper textures that normally don't transfer well. This technique also picks up subtle textures.

The only downfall is that the paper curls a little more. To solve this, I use strong adhesive, such as Wonder Tape. I adhere my page accents with eyelets, brads or stitching.

Compare the examples below. I spritzed my cardstock with water for the example on the left. I didn't use water for the example on the right.

To do wet transfer:

1. Tape one edge of your cardstock onto the texture. *Lightly* mist a 4" section on the side of the cardstock that faces the template. You don't want the side you rub to be wet.

2. Rub the back carefully with the Empressor tool from Chatterbox. The paper will mold easily into the texture. Proceed carefully—the cardstock will tear more easily.

3. Work in small sections and repeat until entire area is embossed.

4. Let dry completely before enhancing.

Cardstock spritzed beforehand with water

Cardstock not spritzed beforehand with water

the giver

Caleb, do you know what you did today? You came home from your Valentine's party with a packet full of candy. When Chandler woke up from his nap he wanted some of your candy. You offered him a sucker. He didn't want it so you offered him another one. He didn't want that one either—so you voluntarily handed him the *entire* packet. He instantly grabbed out a large bag that had 3 mini candy bars and some hearts in it. I wondered what your reaction would be. Without *any* hesitation you said, "It's alright. He can have those." WOW! You know, I'd be amazed if this was a one-time thing, but it actually happens quite frequently. (Since you are a kid with extreme emotions though, we sometimes see the opposite reaction too.) But I've never seen a kid share so selflessly so often. I cannot tell you how much I love it! What a great kid you are, Caleb. ♥ Mommy

Page by Darcee Thompson. **Supplies** *Embossing templates:* Carolee's Creations; *Computer fonts:* CK Letter Home (title), Becky Higgins' "Creative Clips & Fonts" CD; CK Hustle (journaling), "Fresh Fonts" CD, *Creating Keepsakes; Chalk:* Craf-T Products; *Transparency:* Pockets on a Roll, F & M Enterprises; *Brads:* Making Memories. *Idea to note:* Darcee sanded the back of the transparency to give it an opaque look.

Glazed Transfer

Like the look of glazed transfer? Here's how to create it. See facing page for results.

Brush a layer of Crystal Lacquer on your cardstock and let it dry completely.

Brush a thin layer of pigment powder directly on the template.

Tape your cardstock to the template with the lacquer facing down, then emboss your cardstock.

Spray the texture with fixative to set the pigment powder.

Brush excess powder into a jar and wash your template.

t o e n a i l

As I don't have any girls I have to indulge in girlie things every now and again. So when I see Camille (age 3) I let her paint my toenails. I usually end up with as much polish on my toes as I do on my toenails, (yes, she is left handed) but I don't care because she is so cute to watch. I wish I could say that she is getting better, but this picture proves that I need to let her practice more often! And even though I hate to admit it, it is just fun to do little girl things every once in a while! Journaling and Photo 7-03.

Page by Darcee Thompson.
Supplies *Computer font:* Andrew Script, downloaded from the Internet; *Embossing tool:* Hot Boss, Carolee's Creations; *Embossing templates:* Carolee's Creations; *Paper glaze:* Crystal Lacquer, Stampin' Up!; *Pigment powder:* Pearl-Ex, Jacquard Products; *Snaps and letter tiles:* Making Memories; *Conchos:* Scrapworks; *Leafing pen and fixative:* Krylon.

Apply Rub-ons

For an easy-to-create option, apply metallic rub-ons or chalk to your transferred texture. Rub gently so you don't compromise the texture. Try blending different colors for a variegated look.

Card by Darcee Thompson. **Supplies** *Texture template:* Carolee's Creations; *Metallic rub-ons:* Craf-T Products; *Pen:* Zig Millennium, EK Success; *Other:* Thread and brads.

Experiment with Papers

Don't limit your paper to cardstock. Experiment with different papers, such as velvet and even metal sheets. See the examples that follow.

Velvet. Transferring texture onto velvet paper creates a stunning effect. You don't need to rub very hard—just rub in several directions to avoid rubbing lines.

Pages by Darcee Thompson. **Supplies** *Computer font:* CK Typeset, Becky Higgins' "Creative Clips & Fonts" CD, *Creating Keepsakes; Velvet paper:* SEI; *Embossing powder:* Stampendous!; *Embossing template:* Carolee's Creations; *Transparency:* Pockets on a Roll, F & M Enterprises; *Embossing tool:* Hot Boss, Carolee's Creations.

Page by Darcee Thompson. **Supplies** *Textured cardstock:* Bazzill Basics; *Velvet paper:* SEI; *Pop dots:* Therm O Web; *Computer font:* CK Constitution, "Fresh Fonts" CD, *Creating Keepsakes; Chalk:* Craf-T Products; *Colored pencils:* Prismacolor, Sanford; *Fibers:* Stitches, Making Memories; *Texture template:* Carolee's Creations; *Stamping tool:* Hot Boss, Carolee's Creations.

I don't know where life is taking you, but I do know what you are taking into life: compassion, creativity, determination, intelligence, spontaneity and integrity.

Metal sheets. You can also transfer texture onto thin metal sheets. Simply use a dowel instead of an embossing tool. You can even use pigment powder in your template. Or, apply metallic rub-ons or heated embossing powder for a more topical look.

Page by Darcee Thompson. **Supplies** *Letter stamps:* Hero Arts; *Stamping ink:* Fresca, Stampa Rosa; *Nailheads:* BeadDazzled; *Fibers:* Art Sanctum, Fiber Scraps and On The Surface; *Embossing template:* Carolee's Creations; *Computer font:* LainieDay, downloaded from the Internet; *Embroidery floss:* JP Coats; *Embossing powder:* Stampendous!; *Other:* Metal sheet.

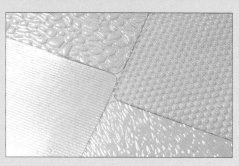

Transfer Options

Looking for textures to transfer? Like Darcee, you can rub the texture from the inside of a freezer at your local home improvement store or from an office ceiling tile. Or, you can check out these manufacturers for more convenient options:

Carolee's Creations • *www.carolees.com*

Fiskars • *www.fiskars.com*

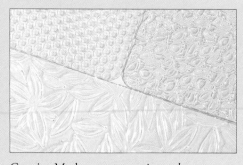

Creative Mode • *www.creativemode.com*

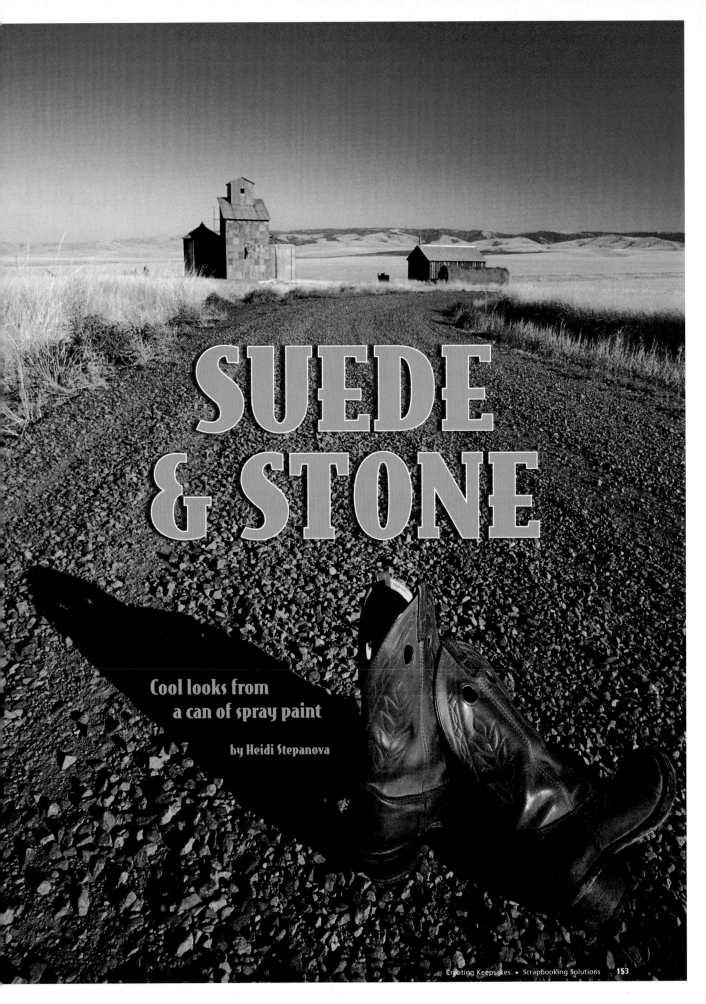

SUEDE & STONE

Cool looks from
a can of spray paint

by Heidi Stepanova

AS THE ONLY WOMAN IN A HOUSE where even the cats are male, I'm always looking for ways to add masculine touches to my pages. Imagine my delight when I stumbled across the new Make It Suede! and Make It Stone! spray paints from Krylon. After all, what's more masculine than leather and stone?

Spray paint has since become one of my many obsessions. It's versatile (it comes in a variety of colors and textures), inexpensive (a can costs less than a package of cardstock), and widely available (check your local craft, hardware or hobby chain).

Many of today's new paints are archivally safe (see "The Safety of Spray Paints" below), quick to apply, fast-drying, and usable on a variety of surfaces. Here's how to create cool suede and stone looks for the "big guy" and "little guy" in your life!

Tips for Applying Spray Paint

Before you press the nozzle, optimize your results with the following tips:

- Always work in a well-ventilated area. Protect the area surrounding your project with a disposable material such as old newspapers or butcher paper.

- Consistency can vary among types and colors of paint. Spray a test paper first to get a feel for the density of coverage.

- To avoid uneven coverage, start your spray several inches outside of your project. Move the can with wide sweeping strokes across your project, going outside of the edges with each stroke, until your project is evenly covered.

- To avoid pools or drips of paint, apply several light coats instead of one heavy coat. If your coat is uneven or too heavy, you have a few options for correcting it. Try wiping off the excess immediately with a paper towel and respraying your piece. (Since the paints are textured they will usually cover any minor wipe marks you create.) If you are working with clay or cardstock, you can always flip it over and spray the back.

  Please note: These corrections can only be done once before the clay, paper or cardstock become too moist. In a worst-case scenario, try leaving the project lying flat until the paint dries to avoid drips.

- If you make a mistake spraying your clay or stamping your image, try reworking the clay until the paint mixes in. Roll the clay out and start over. You may end up with a beautiful color and texture that you decide to keep instead of respraying!

The Safety of Spray Paints

Many spray paints are not archivally safe—they contain ingredients that make them acidic. Krylon, however, has been creating preservation-minded products for over 50 years. The company's products are even used to preserve priceless artwork in museums.

Archivally safe products in the Krylon family include the pH neutral Make It Suede! and Make It Stone! sprays, the company's leafing pens, webbing spray, glitter spray, brush-on paints, paint pens, stained-glass color and premium metallics. To find out more about Krylon products, visit the *www.krylon.com* web site.

suede

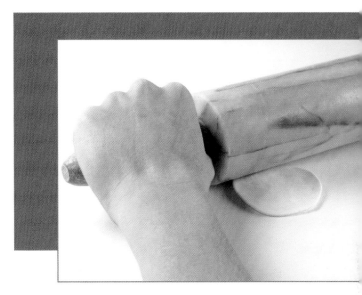

I LOVE THE LOOK OF LEATHER, especially embossed leather. Unfortunately, real leather is often thick and heavy, and the processes used to treat it leave the leather acidic. Krylon's Make It Suede! paints avoid these problems by creating a faux leather finish that's thin, non-acidic and ultra light-weight.

Want to create an embossed leather look for your scrapbook? It's easy—all you need is Make It Suede! paint by Krylon, Makin's Clay by Provo Craft, a rubber stamp and a brown inkpad. Follow these steps:

1 Roll a piece of clay to 1/8" thick. I prefer Makin's Clay, which is more flexible and "forgiving" than other brands. *Note:* Avoid using Sculpey clays, which can damage the spray paint during their required baking process.

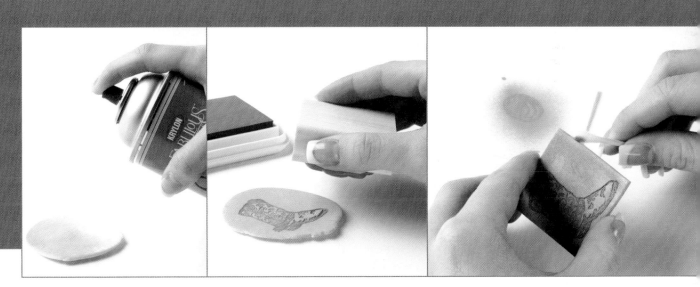

2 Spray an even coat of Make It Suede! over the clay until its color is no longer visible. Generally, this only takes 2–3 passes with a very light touch on the can nozzle.

3 Let the spray paint dry (about five minutes) until it's no longer shiny and feels dry to the touch. Ink your rubber stamp and press it firmly into the clay. The dried paint will keep the clay from sticking to your stamp.

Apply a gentle rocking motion to completely stamp the image, then remove the stamp by "peeling" it from top to bottom. Your clay may curl a little, but lightly patting your hand on the surface will smooth it out again without disturbing your image.

4 Trim the outside edge to the shape you want, then let the clay dry. (Makin's Clay is an air-dry clay that takes a few hours to dry at this thickness. As soon as the piece is dry enough to maintain its shape, you can continue finishing it.) To finish the exposed edges, spray a small pool of paint onto scrap paper and use a cotton swab or brush to apply it to the exposed edges.

Note: If the shade of paint you have on hand doesn't match your layout, chalk it if desired. This highlights the texture and changes the color.

We bought the hat and horse for $2 when the neighbors across the street had a yardsale. It took you a bit to get the hobby horse figured out, but you loved being a cowboy.

COWBOY

For Your Little Guy | Cowboy

Page by Heidi Stepanova. **Supplies** *Spray paint:* Make It Suede! Textured Paint, Krylon; *Clay and texture plates:* Makin's, Provo Craft; *Patterned paper:* K & Company; *Fiber:* Treasured Memories; *Punch:* EK Success; *Rubber stamps:* Hampton Art and Stampabilities; *Word tile:* Die Cuts with a View; *Stamping ink:* ColorBox, Clearsnap; *Chalk:* Craf-T Products; *Walnut ink:* Magic Scraps; *Buffing piece:* AAMCO, *Dimensional adhesive:* Glossy Accents, Ranger Industries; *Other:* Nailhead.

Tip: To create the creased look of old leather, wait until the clay is nearly dry and gently bend it in a few places. (Makin's Clay remains flexible after drying.) Highlight the creases with chalk.

With all the tools my dad has, its hard to imagine he might not have the right tool for a job, and have it close. As long as I can remember, he's been fixing things and building houses, and he's accumulated a lifetime of tools. There is a running joke in our family about these tools. According to my mom, who has spent her entire married life in houses being remodeled, but never a house that is finished being remodeled, whenever she asks my dad to fix something, he never has the right tool for the job. 12/03

For Your Big Guy

Never the Right Tool

Page by Heidi Stepanova. **Supplies** *Spray paint:* Make It Suede! Textured Paint, Krylon; *Clay:* Makin's, Provo Craft; *Patterned paper:* Real Life; *Alphabet stamps:* Making Memories and Hampton Art; *Glove stamp:* Toybox Art; *Gold pen:* Pigma Micron, Sakura; *Chalk:* Craf-T Products; *Stamping ink:* ColorBox, Clearsnap; *Other:* Charms.

Tip: To create the look of raw leather, add texture by rolling your clay (see Step 1 on page 155), then spraying a light coat of Make It Stone! White Onyx Textured Paint before you spray the Make it Suede! paint (see Step 2). *Note:* You do not need to wait for the stone paint to dry before applying the suede paint.

stone

Love the look of etched stone but afraid of extra bulk and weight? Put your worries aside! It's easy to mimic the etched elegance. Be sure to use a firmer touch when stamping your image so the texture of the stone paint is flattened and your ink can adhere evenly.

Follow the same steps described for creating embossed suede accents, but substitute a Make It Stone! Textured Paint and use a solvent-based black inkpad.

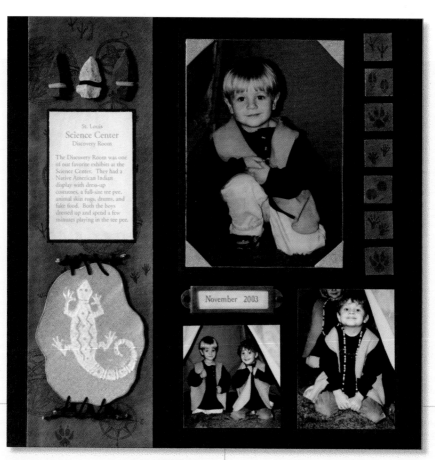

For Your Little Guy

Science Center

Page by Heidi Stepanova. **Supplies** *Spray paint:* Make It Suede! Textured Paint, Krylon; *Clay:* Makin's, Provo Craft; *Bookplate and date stamp:* Making Memories; *Rubber stamps:* Hero Arts, Stampabilities and Stampin' Up!; *Stamping ink:* ColorBox, Clearsnap; *Fiber:* Treasured Memories; *Stickers:* Mrs. Grossman's; *Computer font:* Times New Roman, Microsoft Word; *Chalk:* Craf-T Products; *Other:* Arrowheads.

Tip: To create a negative stamped image, avoid waiting until your paint dries completely. Instead, allow it a few minutes to set up, then stamp the paint with an un-inked stamp. The paint will adhere to your stamp and be lifted away. Be prepared to clean your stamp immediately with a solvent-based stamp cleaner (I like StazOn Cleaner).

October 2003

I love this picture of my dad. It looks like he's standing in the middle of a busy, bustling city street. In truth, he's standing on Broadway in our small rural town on the only day of the year when the streets fill with people—the day of the kids Halloween parade.
Dad had the chance to move to a city, though. When he graduated college, he had a good job offer from Procter & Gamble that would have meant moving to a city and good benefits. This was the job he'd gone to college for, so why'd he stay? My dad had a high number for the draft for the Vietnam war and knew he'd have to serve and leave my mom behind. Plus Mom + Dad knew they wanted kids. So they stayed and now dad visits the city to buy supplies for his business. But really he's a country boy.

For Your Big Guy

City Slicker

Page by Heidi Stepanova. **Supplies** *Spray paint:* Make It Stone! Textured Paint, Krylon; *Clay:* Makin's, Provo Craft; *Patterned paper:* 7 Gypsies; *Metal mesh and screw snaps:* Making Memories; *City stamp:* Paper Candy; *Computer fonts:* Times New Roman, Microsoft Word; CK Bella, "The Art of Creative Lettering" CD, *Creating Keepsakes; Silver pen:* Pigma Micron, Sakura; *Stamping ink:* StazOn, Tsukineko.

Other Uses for Spray Paint

One of the best things about spray paint is that it can be applied to almost any page element. Try spraying any of the following to create coordinating accents:

- Alphabet stickers
- Slide holders
- Bookplates
- Laser cuts
- Photo corners
- Eyelets, nailheads or brads
- Ribbons or thick fibers

A few quick tricks: Press eyelets, brads or nailheads into shipping foam to secure them for spraying. Allow an extra length of ribbon, and tape it down at both ends to a piece of cardboard. For most other light items, temporary adhesive will be enough to hold them in place while spraying.

Tip: Makin's Clay not only remains flexible when dry, but it can also be cut or punched. Add eyelets, brads, or jump rings in the same way you would for cardstock.

9 Accent Ideas

Love the look of leaves, lizards, horses or antique cars? Create memorable accents with a can of Krylon spray and an adventurous spirit. Here's how I created the following.

Supplies *Spray paint:* Make It Suede! Textured Paint, Krylon; *Clay:* Makin's, Provo Craft; *Rubber stamp:* PSX Design; *Stamping ink:* ColorBox, Clearsnap; *Chalk:* Craf-T Products.

Supplies *Spray paint:* Make It Suede! Textured Paint, Krylon; *Clay:* Makin's, Provo Craft; *Stamping ink:* ColorBox, Clearsnap; *Chalk:* Craf-T Products; *Fibers:* Fiber Scraps.

Supplies *Spray paint:* Make It Stone! and Make It Suede! Textured Paint, Krylon; *Clay:* Makin's, Provo Craft; *Rubber stamps:* Hampton Art and Stampabilities; *Stamping ink:* StazOn, Tsukineko; *Embossing powder:* Ranger Industries; *Chalk:* Craf-T Products; *Fibers:* Fiber Scraps; *Ribbon:* Making Memories; *Watch parts:* Scrappin' Fools; *Sticker:* me & my BIG ideas, *Other:* Pewter car.

1

Roll a larger piece of clay and prepare with the step-by-step instructions that come with Berber Make It Suede! paint. Using a rubber stamp with a larger image (at least 3" x 3"), stamp the image with brown paint and allow the piece to dry completely. Flip it over and draw (or trace) a frame on the back. Use scissors to cut out the frame, then finish the exposed edges with chalk.

2

Suede paint can be embossed, but it burns easily. Try lightly burning your paint on purpose! Spray a tag with suede paint and chalk it uniformly. Heat the tag with an embossing gun, watching carefully to make sure the paint doesn't burn while changing to different shades. This effect makes the suede texture more noticeable.

3

Spray paint a piece of cardstock and chalk it to create a background paper. To create the car, follow the step-by-step instructions that come with White Onyx Make It Stone! paint. After the piece is dried completely, rub it very lightly with chalk to make the texture look aged and stand out more.

Supplies *Spray paint:* Make It Stone! Textured Paint and Webbing Paint, Krylon; *Clay:* Makin's, Provo Craft; *Patterned papers:* K & Company and Anna Griffin; *Stamping ink:* StazOn, Tsukineko; *Mesh:* Robin's Nest; *Paper clips:* Making Memories; *Nailheads:* Scrappin' Fools; *Rubber stamps:* Stampabilities; *Mica powder:* Pearl-Ex, USArtQuest; *Rhinestones:* Mrs. Grossman's; *Fibers:* Fiber Scraps.

Supplies *Spray paint:* Make It Suede! Textured Paint, Krylon; *Clay:* Makin's, Provo Craft; *Pen:* Slick Writer, American Crafts; *Chalk:* Craf-T Products; *Fibers:* Treasured Memories; *Beads and feathers:* Crafts, Etc.; *Other:* Arrowhead. *Idea to note:* Heidi drew the bear freehand.

Supplies *Spray paint:* Make It Stone! Textured Paint, Krylon; *Clay:* Makin's, Provo Craft; *Stamp:* Stampabilities; *Stamping ink:* StazOn, Tsukineko; *Computer font:* CK Script, "The Best |of Creative Lettering" CD Combo, *Creating Keepsakes; Chalk:* Craf-T Products; *Fibers:* Fiber Scraps; *Sand dollar:* Magic Scraps; *Beads:* Crafts, Etc., *Other:* Craft wire.

4

To make the stone accents, prepare a piece of clay using the step-by-step instructions that come with the gold Make It Stone! Textured Paint. To lighten the color so the stone paint matches the stamped images on the patterned paper, spray it with Krylon's Workable Fixatif. Brush with Pearl-Ex while the fixatif is still wet.

5

Spray the tag with Berber Make It Suede! paint and let the paint dry completely. Darken the tag color with chalk, then spray with Krylon's Workable Fixatif. Lightly distress the edges with sandpaper.

6

Evenly spray a tag with Gold Make It Stone! Textured paint. Stamp a palm tree, then use chalk to color the tree.

Supplies *Spray paint:* Make It Stone! Textured Paint, Krylon; *Gold leafing pen:* Krylon; *Clay:* Makin's, Provo Craft; *Fibers:* Fiber Scraps; *Snaps:* Chatterbox; *Charms:* Embellish-It.

Supplies *Spray paint:* Make It Suede! Textured Paint, Krylon; *Clay:* Makin's, Provo Craft; *Rubber stamps:* Stampin' Up! and Hampton Art; *Stamping ink:* StazOn, Tsukineko; ColorBox, Clearsnap; *Chalk:* Craf-T Products; *Eyelets:* Making Memories; *Other:* Twine.

Supplies *Spray paint:* Make It Stone! and Make It Suede! Textured Paint, Krylon; *Clay:* Makin's, Provo Craft; *Rubber stamp:* Stampin' Up!; *Stamping ink:* StazOn, Tsukineko; *Chalk:* Craf-T Products; *Fibers:* Treasured Memories; *Beads:* Crafts, Etc.

7

To create the two-tone look, use temporary adhesive to mask off a portion of the tag. If the tag color is dark, a lighter color of paint may require more than one coat.

To create the look of stars, use a very light spray of White Onyx Make It Stone! paint, sprayed about 16" from the cardstock. Cut the sun "rays" from a piece of cardstock, then spray them with Gold Make It Stone! paint.

Note: The metal accents on this tag were originally shiny and four different colors. Heidi changed the color and look with Krylon's gold and silver leafing pens.

8

Follow the step-by-step instructions that come with the spray paint, then chalk it to look rustic. Save your scraps for little accent pieces you may need later. Punch and adhere the circle around the tag opening. Cut and stamp an accent bar from a dry piece of scrap.

9

This lizard shows the effect of using a heavy coat of Make it Stone! White Onyx textured paint when creating a raw leather look. Follow the step-by-step directions for preparing and stamping the clay. Because of the thick coat of stone spray, let the stone paint dry to the touch before spraying with suede paint. ❤

Make Your Own Fake Dog Tags

Dog tags are one of the latest embellishments to hit scrapbook pages en masse. You can purchase pre-stamped metallic tags, or use metal stamps to stamp your own words onto copper or aluminum tags.

Finding the perfect pre-stamped tag can be a challenge, and purchasing the supplies can get costly. Here's an easy, cost-effective way to make tags using the supplies you likely have on hand. All it takes is a clear embossing pad, silver embossing powder, a heat gun, alphabet stamps and cardstock.

❶ Holding the embossing pad upside down, press it onto a piece of cardstock to create a rectangle. (A thicker piece of cardstock will lend a more realistic thickness to the tag.)

❷ Sprinkle the area with silver embossing powder and shake the excess powder back into the container. Melt the powder with your heat gun.

❸ After the area cools, apply another layer of ink and embossing powder, then reheat. Repeat the process two more times to create four layers.

❹ Select the letter stamps you want and, using one hand, hold the "word" of stamps. (I squeeze the word between my thumb and forefinger.) Using the other hand, take the heat gun and heat the center of the embossed area until it begins to liquefy.

❺ Press the "word" into the melted area. Without removing the stamps, allow the area to cool. After 30–40 seconds, gently lift the stamps. The impression should look like a "punched" metal word.

❻ Cut around the word and punch a hole to create a tag. You can use an actual tag as a template or create your own shape. You can find inexpensive chains at a hardware store.

Here are a few additional tips:

◆ Use an old magazine or a thick layer of newspaper under your work area to protect your work surface.

◆ If you make a mistake, reheat the area and try again. Small imperfections will make the tag look more realistic.

◆ If embossing powder melts to your rubber stamps, let the stamps cool, then carefully pick the pieces off with your fingernails.

◆ As a variation, try stamping images rather than words.

—Nicole Keller, Rio Hondo, TX

Editor's note: To prevent melted powder from sticking to your stamps, ink the stamps before pressing them in the embossing powder. For an extra dimension, try colored ink.

Create custom dog-tag embellishments with embossing powder and rubber stamps. *Samples by Nicole Keller.* **Supplies** *Embossing powder:* Mark Enterprises, Stampendous!; *Rubber stamps:* PSX Design and Stamp Craft.

GREAT IMPOSTERS

Mimic metal, twigs and more!

by Denise Pauley

When I was a little girl, I enjoyed grocery shopping with my mother. The appeal wasn't the candy aisle, the toys, and certainly not the fruits and vegetables. It was the row of gumball machines—the place to get a little treat just before we walked out the sliding glass doors.

My favorite? The machine that dispensed imitation gemstone rings in cute plastic capsules. It didn't matter that the "diamond" was a dud or the "ruby" wasn't real—I loved the look of those rings and thought they were just as good as the genuine articles.

I never would have guessed that, years later, I'd like imitations again, not to put on my finger, but on my scrapbook pages!

Although I love to use unconventional accents such as wire and beads on my layouts, many scrapbookers question their archival soundness. They wonder about the effect that excessively dimensional items could have on layouts over time. Good news! With a little effort, many of these embellishments can be mocked or mimicked. You can include versions of them on your pages and feel assured they're safe for your scrapbooks.

Whether it's creating faux objects from archivally safe materials or in a way that makes them less bulky, you'll soon find that imposters can look remarkably like the originals. Although re-creating an accent is much more labor intensive than simply using the "real thing," if you'd like to try a new look or experiment with an old favorite, read on. You just might find a way to achieve the "wow" without the worry!

Charmed, I'm sure.

For such little objects, charms can certainly add flair to your layouts. But if you're reluctant to include metal objects on your pages, design your own without the danger! For each "charm," emboss a small shape onto metallic paper, trim closely around the edges, then raise the shape with a pop dot for realistic dimension (Figure 1). Another method? Use punches on metallic paper and add detail with an embossing stylus.

Tinker with tags.

Whether they're used for titles, accents or cards, tags are all the rage. And one of the most popular types, the round, metal-rimmed variety, is easily mimicked with silver metallic paper and cardstock. Simply punch a circle out of white cardstock, mat with silver, and use a mini circle punch to create the hole through which to thread fibers, floss or more. The ability to design tags of any size and color is an added benefit of this technique, which Wendy Anderson of Heber City, Utah, used to create a fun title for her "Reach" layout in Figure 2.

Nearly nails.

To bring a rustic look to her layout without the threat of actual rust, Cindy Schow of Cardston, Alberta, Canada, simply used metallic paper to create the "nails" on her terrific title block. Though it's just a small touch, the addition works well when combined with the sign's woodgrain look created with cardstock, chalk and pens (Figure 3).

Fake-out fasteners.

Although eyelets and brads can serve as functional fasteners, sometimes they're solely decorative accents. If your layout needs a little something but you don't feel like hammering eyelets or adding the bulk of brads, try inventing some imitations out of cardstock. Mary Larson of Chandler, Arizona, spruced up her page mat and title block with "eyelets" created by double-punching silver metallic cardstock with ⅛" and ¼" circle punches (Figure 4). Nicole Keller of Rio Hondo, Texas, designed her own "brads" in custom colors by punching a mini circle from cardstock, then adding dimension with chalk and a bit of pen work (Figure 5).

Figure 1. Design your own charming accents by dry-embossing metallic paper. *Page by Denise Pauley.* **Supplies** *Gold paper:* Canson; *Computer fonts:* Tempus Sans and Mistral, Microsoft Word; *Embossing templates:* American Crafts (large sun), Lasting Impressions for Paper (swirl sun), source unknown (solid sun); *Fiber:* On the Surface; *Chalk:* Craf-T Products.

Figure 2. Now that you can create your own, there's nothing to keep you from trying metal-rimmed tags! *Page by Wendy Anderson.* **Supplies** *Patterned paper:* Mustard Moon; *Metallic paper:* Accu-Cut Systems; *Letter stickers:* Making Memories; *Silver gel pen:* American Crafts; *Other:* Red crochet thread.

Figure 3. Put away that hammer and pick up a circle punch to include nails on a layout. *Pages by Cindy Schow.* **Supplies** *Patterned paper:* Karen Foster Design; *Antiqued silver foil paper:* Source unknown; *Computer font:* Saloon, Print Shop, Broderbund; *Hole punch:* Marvy Uchida; *Chalk:* Craf-T Products; *Pens:* Zig Writers, EK Success; *Hemp:* Darice; *Pop dots:* All Night Media.

Figure 4. Mimic the ever-popular eyelet and design accents that add interest to your layouts. *Page by Mary Larson.* **Supplies** *Vellum:* Paper Adventures; *Metallic paper for eyelets:* Accu-Cut Systems; *Computer fonts:* Smash (title) and Noisebaby (journaling), downloaded from the Internet; *Circle punches:* Family Treasures and McGill; *Chalk:* Craf-T Products.

Figure 5. Metallic or matte, pearl or primary, make fake brads of all sizes, colors and shapes. *Page by Nicole Keller.* **Supplies** *Heart punch:* EK Success; *Scissors:* Deckle edge, Fiskars; *Fibers:* On the Surface; *Pop dots (for paper punches):* All Night Media; *Pen:* Pigma Micron, Sakura; *Computer font:* CK Primary, "The Art of Creative Lettering" CD, *Creating Keepsakes. Idea to note:* Nicole used her sister's sweater vest as inspiration for her striped page accent.

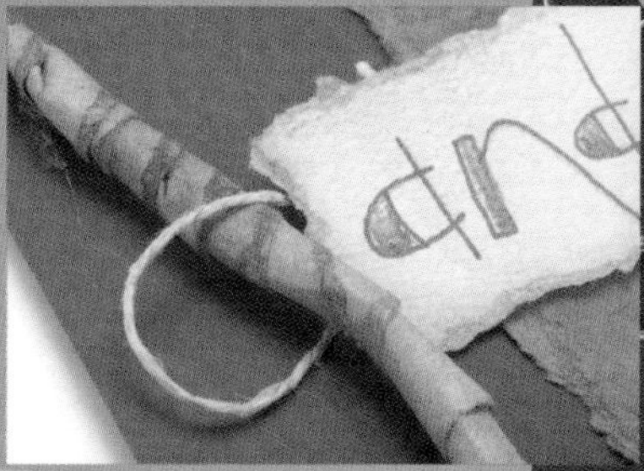

Figure 6. Put an archivally safe twist on twigs by creating them from cardstock. *Page by Darcy Christensen.* **Supplies** *Green leaf paper:* Source unknown; *Colored pencils:* Prismacolor, Sanford; *Chalk:* Craf-T Products; *Title letters:* Handwritten CK Breeze font by Becky Higgins, October 2001 issue of *Creating Keepsakes;* *Other:* Jute and handmade paper "twigs."

A
WdlK
and d
TdlK
and

A morning hike in the beautiful Uintah mountains was a perfect time for Arizona uncle Kent to get caught up with Oregon nephew, Tayler. I was behind them on the trail and looked up to see this perfect shot.
July, 2001

Always &

Figure 7. Fool an oyster with this string of pearls. *Example by Denise Pauley.* **Supplies** *Computer font:* Amazone BT, Microsoft Word; *Liquid Pearls:* Ranger Industries; *Other:* Pearl paper and doily.

Figure 8. Use metallic paper to offer the illusion of glitter without the flurry of stray flakes. *Example by Denise Pauley.* **Supplies** *Gold paper:* one heart … one mind (matte), source unknown (sparkle); *Handmade paper:* Black Ink; *Computer font:* Bickley Script, Microsoft Word; *Fiber:* Rubba Dub Dub.

Figure 9. Producing your own alphabet beads is as easy as A-B-C. *Page by Denise Pauley.* **Supplies** *Silver paper:* Canson; *Vellum:* The Paper Company; *Computer fonts:* CK Script, "The Best of Creative Lettering" CD Combo, *Creating Keepsakes*; Garamouche, downloaded from Internet; *Punches:* EK Success (small square), Fiskars (small circle); *Fiber:* On the Surface; *Pop dots:* All Night Media.

Try your hand at a few of these fun looks and your embellishments could fool the trained eye.

Fool Mother Nature.

Have you ever wanted to add a rustic touch to your page *without* your photos getting quite so close to nature? To create faux twig accents for her layout (Figure 6), Darcy Christensen of Tucson, Arizona, cut strips of tan cardstock and chalked them with brown, rust and black. She then cut pipe cleaners to the desired length (you can also use wire), bent them slightly for a more natural look, and wrapped the pipe cleaners tightly with the chalked paper strips. Darcy used glue dots to hold the "twigs" at each end and secure them to her page. (Double-stick tape will also work.)

Cultured pearls.

For a touch of elegance that can enhance layouts of blessed events, design a string of pearls without the bulk of the real thing. Simply drop tiny dabs of White Opal Liquid Pearls across your cardstock, slightly dragging the applicator after each "pearl" to create the look of string (Figure 7). Or, for a more uniform look, create pearls by punching mini circles from glossy pearl paper and raising them slightly off the page with pop dots.

All that glitters.

Although a touch of glitter can add glitz and glamour to your layout, an ongoing concern is that stray particles could dislodge from your design and damage precious photos. Don't fret! A quick and easy way to capture the look of glitter without stressing over the strays is to use sparkly metallic paper or holographic foil to create titles, accents, mats and more (Figure 8). Raise your "glittered" object on mini pop dots. Or, dry-emboss around the edges to give the added impression of glitter that's been sprinkled and dried over adhesive.

Easy as ABC.

Pewter alphabet beads are a funky way to punch up a title, caption or journaling block. But the dimension they add to a layout can be a little daunting for fans of flat pages.

For a fun takeoff on the look, use a computer to print your title on metallic paper, leaving plenty of space between each letter. Dry-emboss a square around each letter (you can create your own embossing "template" with a small square punch and cardstock) and trim close to the edge. Add string and raise with pop dots to complete the look (Figure 9). You can even use this technique, along with wood veneer, to design Scrabble tile look-alikes.

Make a mesh.

Metal mesh or screening can add a graphic yet elegant touch to your layouts. A subtle, metal-free version is easily obtained with a gray pen (you can use a silver gel pen for an even more metallic look) and straight-edge ruler (Figure 10). You can also use your computer to create a grid pattern and print it in light gray on your cardstock!

Heavy metal.

Achieve the sharp look of sheet metal without actual sharpness. Emboss die cuts and other accents with platinum, gold or bronze Ultra Thick Embossing Enamel, using several layers to achieve a smooth surface. The results look just like pieces punched from metal (Figure 11).

Easily embossed.

If you'd prefer not to heat-emboss, you can try a workaround. Use a glue pen to either trace or free-hand some lettering, a design or object, then allow the glue to dry until it's tacky. Cover with a strip of foil, rub gently, then peel off carefully. You're left with a raised, metallic image that looks like it was heat-embossed!

Add interest to your designs by varying the amount of glue or the manner in which you apply it to create images of varying thickness and texture (Figure 12). You can also use this technique to create faux wire by drawing a thin line with your glue pen.

Try your hand at a few of these fun looks and your embellishments could fool the trained eye. The next time you see a cool, 3-D page accent, look again. It just might be a great imposter! ♥

Figure 10. The look of metal mesh is now at your fingertips! *Example by Denise Pauley.* **Supplies** *Pressed flower stickers:* Botanicals, SEI, Inc.; *Pen:* Zig Calligraphy, EK Success; *Other:* Corrugated paper.

Figure 11. Make mock metal shapes with the help of bronze Ultra Thick Embossing Enamel. *Example by Denise Pauley.* **Supplies** *Textured paper:* Books by Hand; *Embossing enamel:* Ultra Thick Embossing Enamel, Suze Weinberg, Ranger Industries; *Die cut:* Sizzix, Provo Craft; *Embossing ink:* Dauber Duo, Tsukineko; *Fibers:* Rubba Dub Dub, On the Surface and On the Fringe.

Figure 12. No time to heat-emboss? Use a glue pen and foil to re-create the look in a pinch. *Example by Denise Pauley.* **Supplies** *Foil:* Sunday International; *Rubber stamps:* Impress Rubber Stamps; *Ink pad:* Stampin' Up!; *Pen:* Zig Millennium, EK Success.

The Hazy, Lazy Days Of Summer...

One of my early memories is of my dad singing this song to me:
"I have two little hands that are sticky with goo,
And if you're not careful they will stick to you!"
He had altered the lyrics from this Primary song. Come to think
of it. I think he washed my hands while singing it!

I have two little hands folded snuggly and tight.
They are tiny and weak, yet they know what is right.
During all the long hours till daylight is through,
There is plenty indeed for my two hands to do.

Kind Father I thank thee for two little hands.
And ask thee to bless them till each understands.
That children can only be happy all day.
When two little hands have learned how to obey.

Try faux wax seals as button-like accents on your next scrapbook page. *Sample by Lori Fairbanks.* **Supplies** *Rubber stamp, colored glue sticks and Release Paper:* Embossing Arts Co.; *Stamping ink:* ColorBox, Clearsnap; *Silver cord:* Stampin' Up!; *Computer fonts:* CAC Pinafore, downloaded from the Internet; CK Fun, "The Art of Creative Lettering" CD, *Creating Keepsakes.*

Faux Wax Seals

Would you like to add wax seal accents to a scrapbook page without the seals cracking? Try using Colorful Glue Sticks with your rubber stamps. Because the glue is acid free, the seal is safe for your layout. And when you create the seal on Release Paper, you can easily remove the seal and mount it with a glue pen or glue dots.

Melt the glue sticks with a heat embossing tool or glue gun. If you need just a few seals or want to experiment with colors and techniques, use the heat embossing method:

❶ Snip a ½" piece from the glue stick and place it on a sheet of Release Paper. One glue stick can create eight seals.
❷ Pre-ink your stamp using pigment ink or clear embossing ink and set it aside.
❸ Apply heat until the glue melts. When the glue is partially melted, the glue disc will continue to flatten as it sits.
❹ Gently press the pre-inked stamp into the warm glue disc. Allow it to cool, then remove your stamp. (If you want to redo the seal, snip it into small pieces and reheat it on the Release Paper to create a new disc.)

If you need to make a lot of seals, use a glue gun. Here are some tips for using the glue gun method:

❶ Insert the glue and preheat your glue gun. Pre-ink your rubber stamp and set it aside.
❷ Once the glue begins to ooze from the gun's tip, apply the glue to Release Paper and allow it to cool for 30–60 seconds.
❸ Press the inked stamp into the warm glue. Allow the seal to cool and remove the stamp.
◆ When you create seals using a hot glue gun, you'll need a clear glue stick to "clean" the gun before changing colors. You'll also need to use the entire glue stick once it's been placed in the glue gun. Take advantage of the beautiful marbled effects while you "clean" the glue gun.
◆ For another unique effect, cut the different colored sticks into small pieces and insert them into the glue gun, one after another. If you use several colors of glue sticks, always begin with the lightest color to make color changes easier.

Variations: While the glue disc is hot, sprinkle it with embossing powder—the powder will melt instantaneously. You can also reheat a disc, cover it with embossing powder, remove the excess and heat as usual. Add sparkle by sprinkling glitter or Pearl-Ex into the hot glue; or apply Pearl-Ex and Metallic Rub-ons to dress up finished seals. Seal them with a fixative spray.

—*Sue Settles, Embossing Arts Co.*

This is a moment I want you to remember – a golden, flowery time when you were simply content and happy to be around each other...when you could watch a video agreeably and quietly chatter about the characters or sing along with the songs...when Ryan still got a kick out of wearing Erin's necklaces proudly around the house...when Ryan considered Erin to be the most comfy "chair" he could find...and when Erin didn't mind a bit.

2003 August

M.E.M.O.I.R.L.E.S.

family

CUSTOMIZED

Cork

5 creative ways to add a textural twist

CORK has made its way onto scrapbook pages, and it's a great fit. As a teen I spent many an afternoon arranging and rearranging photos, clippings, buttons and school spirit ribbons on my bulletin board. Cork will always be associated with my memories.

Is it just nostalgia turning cork into a popular page accent? Not at all! Its uses go far beyond the occasional "mock bulletin board" layout. Banish the image of brown, crumbly cork from your mind.

Besides providing texture and dimension with minimal bulk, cork is almost as versatile as cardstock. The new varieties—those designed for crafting and scrapbooking—are durable enough to be stamped and sewn, etched and embossed, painted and punched.

The next time you're creating a cool background or accent, reach for cork. Here are five different ways this versatile medium can give traditional techniques a terrific textural twist.

BY DENISE PAULEY

"THIS MOMENT" *by Denise Pauley.* **Supplies** *Patterned paper:* Creative Imaginations; *Handmade paper:* Provo Craft; *Cork and transparency:* Magic Scraps; *Computer font:* CK Constitution, "Fresh Fonts" CD, *Creating Keepsakes; Foam stamp:* Suzy's Zoo; *Date stamp:* Making Memories; *Stamping ink:* StazOn, Tsukineko; Fresco, Stampa Rosa; *Chalk:* Craf-T Products; *Leafing pen:* Krylon; *Acrylic paint:* Delta Technical Coatings; *Plaque:* Li'l Davis Designs; *Scrabble words:* Limited Edition Rubber Stamps; *Brass frame:* Ink It; *Photo corner:* 7 Gypsies; *Tags:* DMD, Inc.; *Hemp:* Darice; *Other:* Gold leaf flake.

Painting

Brighten the natural look of cork with a swish of metallic paint and gold leafing. If the result is too shiny for the mood of your layout, distress the accents by lightly sanding them and applying ink to the edges and surfaces. The process is simple:

❶ Dip a foam stamp in liquid glue, then carefully press onto the cork.

❷ Let the image dry until tacky, then pat on a thick layer of gold leaf flake.

❸ Allow the flake to dry completely, then use a stiff brush to remove excess leafing.

❹ For added dimension, tear around each flower, then distress the accent a bit with fine-grain sandpaper, ink and chalk.

❺ Adhere your accent to another layer of cork that has been dry brushed with gold acrylic paint.

"FACE TO THE SUNSHINE" *by Nichol Magouirk.* **Supplies** *Patterned papers:* Anna Griffin (striped) and me & my BIG ideas (floral); *Cork:* Magic Scraps; *Letter stickers:* me & my BIG ideas (vintage); Terri Martin (script), Creative Imaginations; *Ribbon, stitched tag and trim:* me & my BIG ideas; *Metal-rimmed tag and buckle charm:* Making Memories; *Walnut ink:* 7 Gypsies; *Tag:* DMD, Inc.; *Embroidery floss:* DMC; *Chalk:* Craf-T Products; *Other:* Hemp.

Stitching

Cork is surprisingly durable and will easily stand up to needlework. Add a cozy, old-fashioned feel to a cork mat with hand-sewn flowers and edges aged with dark brown chalk. To create a beautiful sewn mat, follow these steps:

❶ Cut the cork to create a frame, then chalk the edges.

❷ Stitch the fabric tag to the bottom of the frame.

❸ Hand stitch daisy flowers and stems to the cork frame. (*Tip:* Use a small needle for hand stitching; large needles may crack the cork. For flower and stem accents, use just three of the six strands of floss so it will pass through the cork. Use all six strands to make French knots for the flower centers.)

❹ Mount your picture, then machine stitch the frame to the background.

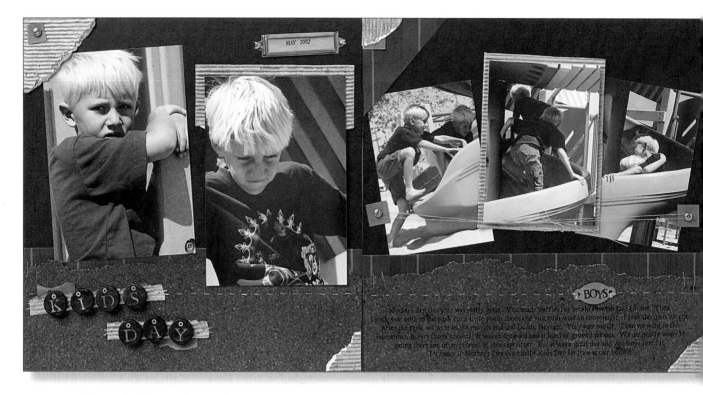

"KIDS DAY" *by Alison Beachem.* **Supplies** *Patterned paper and letter stamps:* PSX Design; *Cork:* Magic Scraps; *Corrugated paper:* DMD, Inc.; *Title letters:* Inspirables, EK Success; *Stamping ink:* StazOn, Tsukineko; *Screw eyelets:* Making Memories; *Acrylic paint:* Delta Technical Coatings; *Walnut ink:* Pinecone Press; *Thread:* Hillcreek Designs; *Other:* Brass plate and staples.

Journaling

Tired of the same old journaling blocks? Send thin cork through your printer to give your words extra impact. For a quick color change and an ultra-rich look, douse the cork with a walnut ink wash.

Hall of Famer Alison Beachem offers the following tip for sending cork through your printer: "Using a removable adhesive, adhere the cork to a piece of cardstock. Place it approximately ½" from the edge to help the printer accept the feed."

Banish the image of brown, crumbly cork from your mind.

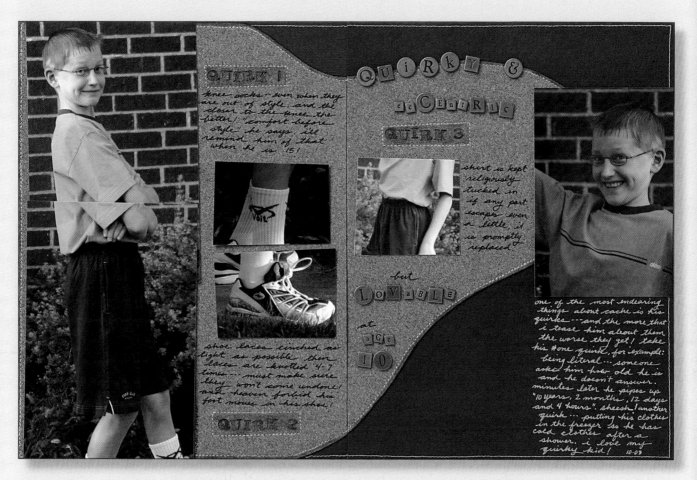

"QUIRK!" *by Darcee Thompson.* **Supplies** *Cork:* Magic Scraps; *Pens:* Sakura and American Craft; *Embossing tool and stamps:* Hot Boss, Carolee's Creations; *Chalk:* Craf-T Products.

Texturing

Cork's flexibility makes it ideal for making impressions. Enhance its texture and highlight journaling by etching key words with a wood-burning tool, then add even more visual interest with machine stitching and a flourish of chalk.

To add stamped texture to cork:

❶ Heat a wood-burning tool. Once the unit is hot, attach the metal stamp.

❷ Let the tool heat for another minute. Test it on a scrap of cork to make sure the tool is hot enough to brand in the letter.

❸ Press the heated metal stamp onto your cork until an impression is made. Use needle-nose pliers to change stamps.

Variation: Use the tip of the wood-burning tool to create lines and other freehand designs. Draw pencil lines on the cork to help guide you.

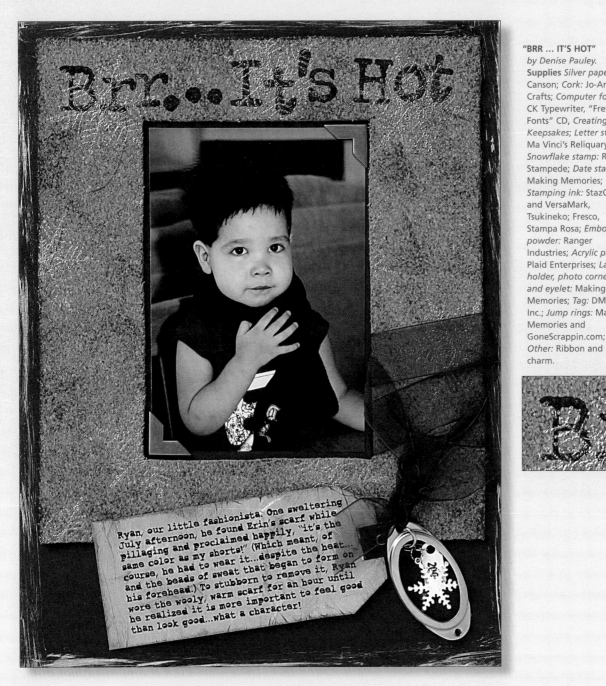

"BRR … IT'S HOT"
by Denise Pauley.
Supplies *Silver paper:*
Canson; *Cork:* Jo-Ann
Crafts; *Computer font:*
CK Typewriter, "Fresh
Fonts" CD, *Creating
Keepsakes; Letter stamps:*
Ma Vinci's Reliquary;
Snowflake stamp: Rubber
Stampede; *Date stamp:*
Making Memories;
Stamping ink: StazOn
and VersaMark,
Tsukineko; Fresco,
Stampa Rosa; *Embossing
powder:* Ranger
Industries; *Acrylic paint:*
Plaid Enterprises; *Label
holder, photo corners
and eyelet:* Making
Memories; *Tag:* DMD,
Inc.; *Jump rings:* Making
Memories and
GoneScrappin.com;
Other: Ribbon and
charm.

Stamping

Use a thick sheet of cork to create an ultra-dimensional photo mat that will still be forgiving in page protectors. Customize the cork with rubber stamps and ink to suit your color and theme. The sheet will stand up to heat embossing without warping or scorching. Try the following:

❶ Trim the photo mat to the desired size (a craft knife works well).

❷ Stamp the snowflake several times in a random pattern, then heat emboss with silver embossing powder.

❸ Lightly brush an inkpad across the edges and surface of the mat for additional color and a "distressed" look.

❹ Stamp your title on the frame. ❤

PATTERNED PERFECTION

Avoid the pitfalls, achieve great looks > BY JANA LILLIE

While shopping recently at a scrapbook store, I showed a friend some patterned paper I love. "You're brave," she said. "Me? I've sworn off patterned paper."

"Really," I said. "Why's that?"

"No matter what I do, I just can't make it look good. My pages end up feeling 'busy.' I'm thinking I'm just not a patterned-paper person."

"Whoa," I said. "Don't be hasty. I was tempted to think the same thing—then I noticed new papers I just couldn't resist. I decided to learn what works and what doesn't. It's not as hard as I thought it might be."

"Maybe you're right," said my friend. "I do love what I'm seeing—I just have a lousy track record. Can you help?" I hope so!

Here's input on how to achieve your best looks yet with patterned paper.

AVOID THE PITFALLS

Patterned paper provides a quick way to add personality to a page, but mixing different colors and patterns can be a bit overwhelming. Here's how to avoid common pitfalls:

PITFALL 1:
The Competing Background

Let's say you're scrapbooking pictures of your dog playing with the neighbor kids. You're tempted to use "dog bone and collar" paper for your page background, but every time you place your photos on the paper, they get lost among all the page elements. How can you stay out of this design "doghouse"?

Try this:
- Use a strip of the torn patterned paper as a border against a coordinating solid paper.
- Mat your photos with solid-colored paper for visual separation. They'll stand out more against the patterned paper.
- Choose pictures with strong focal points and few objects, colors and patterns. Or, include less photos. Says Shauna Berglund-Immel, a designer for Hot Off The Press, "Choose one or two of the best photos to scrapbook. This will help your pages look cleaner and less cluttered."
- Cut out your favorite images and use them as decorative accents. They make great additions to journaling blocks, for example.

PITFALL 2:
The Not-So-Stylish Mix of Styles

You want to mix different patterned papers on a layout, but the results look messy. How can you switch from mish-mash to mesmerizing?

Try this:
- Look at the papers you're planning to use. Are the overall looks complementary, or are you trying to mix, for example, "masculine" papers with "ultra-feminine" papers? Would a stone pattern work with a frilly, antiqued pattern? Probably not!
- Check your colors. Are they complementary, or are you trying to combine colors (such as aquamarine and powder-blue) that don't mix well in either tone or hue?
- Use colors and shades of papers that are pre-coordinated for you.

PITFALL 3:
The Bold Ones

You love the energy a bold pattern can add to a layout, but the last time you used one, your photos and journaling got "zapped" in the process. People were drawn to the pattern and not the photos and journaling.

Try this:
- Mute your bold patterned paper with a vellum overlay.
- Use the paper with photos that are visually simple but strong on color and composition.
- Limit the amount of patterned paper you use. Place smaller pieces where you want to draw extra attention.

ACHIEVE GREAT LOOKS

Once you have the basics of patterned paper down, apply them!

You can create terrific looks like the following.

Supplies *Patterned paper:* Karen Foster Design; *Computer fonts:* Book Antiqua (title), Microsoft Word; 2Peas Hot Chocolate (journaling), downloaded from *www.twopeasinabucket.com; Fiber:* From *www.brownbagfibers.com.*

"Our Cabin"
by Kimberly Lund
Wichita, KS

- Use patterned paper to establish mood and create a sense of drama. Here, Kimberly chose a dark-brown patterned paper to fit with semi-serious journaling about an "otherworldly presence" inside her family's cabin.

- Another trick of Kimberly's? If a paper's pattern has elements that are distracting, position your photos and title blocks to minimize the pattern.

"Our First Weekend"
**by Susan Cobb for
Hot Off The Press**

- To create a distressed look, randomly scuff your patterned paper (see ivory paper here) with fine-grade sandpaper.
- Place a strip of paper behind a photo to help "ground" it and lend a graphic touch.

Supplies *Patterned paper:* Paper Pizazz, Hot Off The Press; *Buttons:* Magic Scraps; *Embroidery floss:* DMC; *Chalk:* Craf-T Products; *Pen:* Zig Writer, EK Success; *Other:* Fine-grade sandpaper.

"Maya"
**by Katrina Lawrence
Provo, UT**

- Add a playful touch with a hint of patterned paper "peeking" from a corner.

Supplies *Patterned paper:* Doodlebug Design; *Frame and flower die cuts:* Polly & Friends, Leeco Industries; *Ribbon:* May Art; *Metal letters:* Making Memories; *Computer font:* EmmaScript, downloaded from the Internet.

"Pool"

by Angelia Wigginton
Belmont, MS

• Head for the border! Add a splash of color and pattern along one side of your page. Repeat the look on a photo mat as well.

Supplies *Patterned paper:* Colors By Design; *Vellum:* The Paper Company; *Metal-rimmed tags:* Making Memories; *Fibers:* From *www.brownbagfibers.com*; *Nailheads:* Jewelcraft; *Stamping ink:* Imprintz; *Letter stamps:* PSX Design; *Computer font:* 2Peas Chicken Shack, downloaded from *www.twopeasinabucket.com*. *Idea to note:* Angelia used nailheads to anchor her fibers along the lines of the patterned paper.

"Sweeter in a Sweater"

by Vivian Smith
Calgary, AB, Canada

• Need a different color or tint on patterned paper? Use a vellum overlay. Here, Vivian turned leftover, pink-flowered paper to a browny orange with a brown overlay.

• Tone down patterned paper with vellum, chalk, metallic rub-ons, watercolors, ink pads or pencil crayons.

Supplies *Patterned paper:* Carolee's Creations (brown with stars), Keeping Memories Alive (brown stripe), Provo Craft (flowered, for flaps), Scrap Happy (brown background); *Vellum:* Provo Craft; *Computer fonts:* CK Elegant (title), "Fresh Fonts" CD, *Creating Keepsakes*; PC Willa (journaling), "Feed the Birds" HugWare CD, Provo Craft; *Buttons:* Making Memories; *Pen:* Zig Scroll & Brush, EK Success.

Supplies *Patterned paper:* Provo Craft; *Rubber stamps:* PSX Design; *Tag die cut:* Sizzix; *Other:* Eyelets and mini brads.

"Big Thunder Mountain"
by Angie Cramer
Redcliff, AB, Canada

- Create a quilted look. First, select your photos, 2-3 colors of solid-colored cardstock, and a stack of patterned paper. Move the pieces around to decide on final placement.
- Incorporate solid-colored cardstock in the design to provide visual "resting spots."

"Fascination"
by Ali Edwards
Eugene, OR

- Cut patterned paper at various angles.
- Separate the pieces evenly. You get an interesting effect *and* a new use for leftover paper scraps!

Supplies *Patterned paper:* Magenta; *Vellum letter stickers:* Mrs. Grossman's; *Pen:* Zig Millennium, EK Success.

Supplies *Patterned paper:* Keeping Memories Alive, Provo Craft and The Paper Patch; *Computer font:* Fontdiner.com, downloaded from the Internet; *Poem:* Downloaded from *www.twopeasinabucket.com.*

"How Do I Love Thee?"
by Jodee Madder
Pittsburgh, PA

- "Stack" leftover strips of coordinating paper to create a decorative background.
- Afraid you'll be dealing with too many colors and patterns? Change your color photo to black and white, then back it partially with a journaling block on solid paper.

Supplies *Patterned paper:* Patchwork Paper Company; *Tree buttons and embroidery floss:* Making Memories; *Letter stickers:* Sonnets by Sharon Soneff, Creative Imaginations; *Computer font:* 2Peas Flea Market, downloaded from *www.twopeasinabucket.com*; *Embossing powder:* Stampendous!; *Ink pad:* Rubber Stampede; *Other:* Date stamp from office supply store.

"Silly Santa"
by Wendy Anderson
Heber, UT

- Use two colors of the same pattern for a page background and accents.
- Tear one piece, then line up the patterns to create one flowing background.

Supplies *Patterned papers:* Paper Pizazz, Penny Black and Provo Craft; *Vellum:* Stamp-It; *Computer font:* Aladdin, downloaded from the Internet; *Rubber stamps:* Close To My Heart, Hero Arts, Inkadinkadoo and Rubberdubbadoo; *Stamping ink:* VersaColor, Tsukineko; *Watercolor ink pad:* Ranger Industries; *Chalk:* Craf-T Products.

"All About Me"
by Nicola Howard
Pukekohe, S. Auckland, New Zealand

Do a little "deconstruction" by scratching and layering your patterned paper for a custom look. Here's how:

1. Select four patterned papers and trim them to the desired size. Use a glue stick to adhere them one on top of the other. Let the paper dry.

2. Scratch holes in the paper with an X-acto knife. This will expose the different layers in different places.

3. Rub sandpaper over the paper as well if desired.

4. Enjoy the results. If you end up with large lumps of torn paper, you can glue them down, let the adhesive dry, then re-scratch them for artistic effect.

Supplies *Patterned paper:* Scrap-Ease; *Hole punch:* Marvy Uchida; *Chalk:* Craf-T Products; *Computer fonts:* CK Indigo (title) and CK Constitution (journaling), "Fresh Fonts" CD, *Creating Keepsakes. Idea to note:* Vivian chose patterned paper that looks similar to the pillow fabric behind her daughter's head.

"Sage"
by Vivian Smith
Calgary, AB, Canada

- Use four pieces of patterned paper to create a "quadrant" on a solid-colored sheet of background paper.
- Chalk opposing blocks of paper (those with pink dots here) to darken them.

Supplies *Patterned paper:* Bo-Bunny Press.

"Card and Torn Frame"
by Joy Candrian
for Bo-Bunny Press

- To add an elegant touch to photos, tear a frame from double-sided patterned paper, then roll back the edges. Note how double-sided paper increases your decorative possibilities.

MORE TIPS FROM READERS

We asked scrapbookers for their best tips on using patterned paper. Here's a quick sampling:

"Whenever I plan to use one or more patterned papers on a layout, I take a color wheel to the store to help me purchase colors that truly complement each other."

—Tracy Kyle, Coquitlam, BC, Canada

"Generally, keep your number of patterns to three or less. Also, practice your scales. When selecting the three patterns, choose one large, dominant pattern (such as a large plaid) and two medium- to small-scale secondary patterns (such as dots)."

—Darcy Christensen, Tucson, AZ

"Can't find a coordinating sheet of patterned paper? Create your own! Simply scan fabric from an actual article of clothing shown in the photo, then print out matching patterned paper."

—Susan Piepol, Rockville, MD

"I follow the same methods used by interior designers. For example, with the dominant-color method, I choose a color in a pattern, then select other patterns that contain the chosen color, usually mixed with a neutral. I place solid-colored paper (in the color of my choice) between the patterns to help my page look crisp and focused."

—Erica Pence, Boynton Beach, FL

"If you create all your scrapbook pages in an 8½" x 11" format but find a sheet of 12" x 12" patterned paper that you love, cut off an 8½" x 11" piece for one page, then use the remaining 3½" strip as an accent on the facing page."

—Ellyn Zinsmeister, Allen, TX

"Bold patterned paper looks best with strong, clear photos that can hold their own against the pattern. Also, a student in one of my classes offered some helpful advice: In most cases, your paper's pattern should not be bigger than the subject's head in your pictures."

—Tracy Miller, Fallston, MD

"I like to use patterned papers that offer additional designs in the same color scheme. Mixing the same colors in coordinating patterns always looks nice, or you can mix different colors of the same patterns. When mixing paper from different companies, I like to go for a monochromatic look and stick with the same color in different patterns.

"Another big help? I always lay my photo or photos directly on top of the patterned paper to see how it looks. This quickly eliminates many paper choices."

—Nichol Magouirk, Dodge City, KS

Supplies *Patterned paper and vellum:* Paper Adventures; *Computer fonts:* David Walker and 2 Peas Distressed, downloaded from *www.two-peasinabucket.com*; *Fibers, flower buttons and flower charm:* Making Memories; *Beads and craft wire:* Westrim Crafts; *Ribbon:* Jo-Ann Crafts; *Slide mount:* From *www.scrapsahoy.com*; *Other:* Heart and square brads.

"Lulu"
by Jordan Stone
Columbia, MO

- Have a bold, bright photo subject? Choose a punchy yet fairly simple paper for your background. The stripes work here, while a more complex pattern might not.
- Jordan chose a non-dominant color (green) for her background paper so the bright blues and yellows would "pop" more visually.

new looks
with letter stickers

Emboss, sand and experiment your way to "wow"

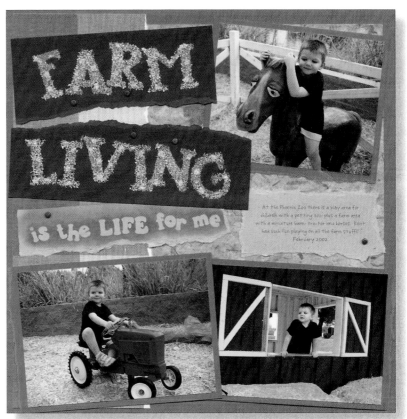

Figure 1. Give letter stickers a country look with straw speckles. *Page by Mary Larson.* **Supplies** *Patterned paper:* Anna Griffin; *Handmade paper:* Source unknown; *Letter stickers:* Renae Lindgren ("Farm Living"), Creative Imaginations; Alphabit-ties ("is the LIFE for me"), Provo Craft; *Brads:* American Tag; *Computer font:* CK Jot, "The Art of Creative Lettering" CD, *Creating Keepsakes.*

RAISE YOUR HAND if you own letter stickers! Aha, just as I thought—most of you do. If you're like me, you bought them to use for quick pages, yet you haven't used them much because you crave looks that are more specialized.

I'm here to show you fun techniques to customize what you own, plus cool new letters that can spice up your pages. While some of the ideas I'll share are quick and easy, others are more advanced. Simply choose what meets your needs.

Sticker Types

First, a refresher on letter sticker types. This is important because not every technique covered here will work with every letter type. Knowing which type of letter

Figure 2. Silver beads soften letter stickers and add texture to a title. *Title by Mary Larson.* **Supplies** *Patterned paper:* O'Scrap!, Imaginations!, Inc.; *Letter stickers:* David Walker, Colorbök ("V"), Mrs. Grossman's ("O"), SRM Press ("L") and The Honey Tree ("E"); *Metallic rub-ons:* Craf-T Products; *Square punch:* Family Treasures; *Brads:* American Tag.

Figure 3. Add swoops of glitter to match the letters for a sparkly title. *Title by Mary Larson.* **Supplies** *Letter stickers and paper:* Flavia by Colorbök; *Other:* Glitter.

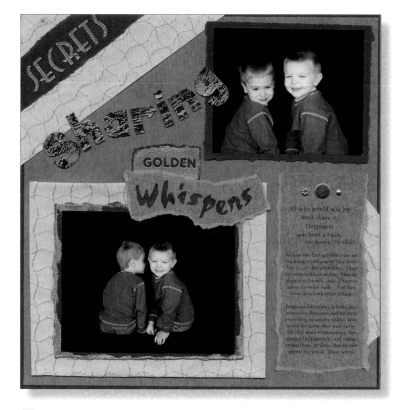

Figure 4. Multiple letter techniques on the same layout add interest and pizzazz. *Page by Mary Larson.* **Supplies** *Patterned paper:* Crafter's Workshop; *Handmade paper:* Source unknown; *Letter stickers:* Sleek ("Secrets") and Sassy ("Whispers"), Shotz, Creative Imaginations; Provo Craft ("Sharing"); Sandylion ("Golden"); *Inkpad and background stamp for "Sharing":* Stampin' Up!; *Embossing powder:* StampCraft; *Computer font:* Garamouche, Impress Rubber Stamps; *Other:* Nailheads.

you're using before you start a technique will save time and frustration. Here's a quick rundown:

◆ **Die cut and paper backed.** These stickers contain no border around the colored part. Examples include Chunky Watercolor by Making Memories, Shotz by Creative Imaginations and Blocky by Provo Craft.

◆ **Die cut and clear backed.** These stickers contain no border (or a very small one) around the colored part. Examples include the David Walker and Flavia lines by Colorbök.

◆ **Die cut and paper bordered.** These stickers contain a white border around the letters. They're also die cut. One example is the Country Alphabet by Debbie Mumm.

◆ **Clear bordered.** These stickers contain a clear border or block around the letters. Examples include the Curly Alphabet from me & my BIG ideas, the Classic Alphabet from Mrs. Grossman's, and letter stickers from Sandylion, SEI and Karen Foster Design.

7 Techniques for More Stylish Stickers

Many letter stickers come in only one color or pattern. While the letter shape or font can be what you're looking for, sometimes you'd like a characteristic to be slightly different. Use the following techniques to change the color or texture and create a perfect fit!

❶ **Overlaying.** With this technique, you change the color or texture of a letter sticker by overlaying it with fun products. Here's how:

a. Roughly cut the letters you want to use away from the sheet, leaving the backing around them.

b. Run each letter sticker face-down through a Xyron machine (I like the 150 model) or apply liquid adhesive. The adhesive should be on top of the letter.

c. Carefully peel the letter sticker from its backing. (A straight pin can help you lift it without damaging the adhesive.) Place the letter sticker on your layout, tapping it down with the straight pin.

d. Sprinkle speckles, beads or glitter on top of the letter sticker, then tap off the excess. You'll get great results like those in Figures 1–3.

❷ **Embossed ink.** With this technique, you use an inkpad or rubber stamp to create embossed letters or reverse letter embossing. I'll share the steps for three quick variations.

◆ Inked and embossed (see "Secrets" and "Whispers" in Figure 4). To create this look:

a. Carefully peel the letter sticker off the sheet. Lightly place the sticker on the end of your pointer finger.

b. Dab the letter sticker on an inkpad until the sticker is coated with ink.

c. Place the inked letter sticker on cardstock, being careful not to disturb the ink. Make sure the sticker is positioned securely enough that embossing powder will not sift underneath.

d. Coat the letter sticker with embossing powder, then set the powder with a heat gun.

e. Carefully peel the letter sticker from the cardstock. Place the letter sticker as desired on your layout.

◆ Stamped and embossed (see "Sharing" in Figure 4). This look is most suited to larger and wider letter stickers. To create it:

a. Choose a stamp (such as a

Figure 5. Mix black and white briefly for a mottled, stone-textured look. *Title by Mary Larson.* **Supplies** *Patterned paper:* Karen Foster Design; *Stickers:* Magenta; *Letter stickers:* K & Company ("Finally") and NRN Designs ("Fall"); *Eyelets:* Making Memories; *Other:* Acrylic paint.

Figure 6. Use fiber and crimped paper to add texture to a layout. *Page by Mary Larson.* **Supplies** *Handmade paper:* Books by Hand; *Letter stickers:* Making Memories ("Wrinkly") and me & my BIG ideas ("Kurt" and "Fingers and Toes"); *Crimper:* Paper Adventures; *Computer font:* CK Toggle, "The Best of Creative Lettering" CD, *Creating Keepsakes;* *Fibers:* Rubba-Dub-Dub, Art Sanctum; *Buttons:* Making Memories; *Brads:* American Tag.

Figure 7. Mix letter sticker sizes and fonts for a custom look. *Title by Mary Larson.* **Supplies** *Patterned paper:* Carolee's Creations; *Handmade paper:* Source unknown; *Letter stickers:* me & my BIG ideas ("Home") and Sandylion ("sweet"); *Chalk:* Craf-T Products; *Inkpad:* Colorbox, Clearsnap.

 Figure 8. Combine twine and crumpled paper for a rough-and-ready outdoor title. *Title by Mary Larson.* **Supplies** *Patterned paper:* Paper Loft; *Letter stickers:* Making Memories; *Other:* Twine and sandpaper.

Figure 9. Embossed paper and metallic rub-ons make an elegant combination. *Title by Mary Larson.* **Supplies** *Embossed paper:* K & Company; *Vellum:* Paper Adventures; *Letter stickers:* Provo Craft ("Autumn") and Sandylion ("leaves"); *Metallic rub-ons:* Craf-T Products.

 **Figure 10.** Plaid paper adds a playful, colorful touch to a school title. *Title by Mary Larson.* **Supplies** *Patterned paper:* Mustard Moon; *Letter stickers:* Stickopotamus, EK Success; *Wooden pencil:* Provo Craft; *Chalk:* Craf-T Products.

Figure 11. Glittery, layered letters lend a festive touch to holiday titles. *Title by Mary Larson.* **Supplies** *Patterned paper:* Treehouse Designs; *Letter stickers:* Paper Adventures ("Holiday") and Sandylion ("Wishes"); *Rectangle punch:* McGill.

background or texture stamp) that has a small pattern.

b. Carefully peel your letter sticker off the sheet.

c. Ink the rubber stamp, then place the letter sticker upside-down on the upside-down stamp, or temporarily adhere your letter sticker and stamp it.

d. Move the letter sticker to a scrap of cardstock and lightly adhere the letter. (Use a straight pin to tap it down.)

e. Sprinkle the letter with embossing powder, then shake off the excess. Set the powder with a heat gun.

f. Carefully peel the letter from

the cardstock. Place the letter sticker as desired on your layout.

◆ Reverse letter embossing (see "Golden" in Figure 4). This technique is great for using small letter stickers in any color. (I even used some small letters that came with a child's sticker set!) As shown in Figure 1, you can also create this look with chalk.

To create the look in Figure 4:

a. Peel letter stickers off the sheet and position them in a permanent place on the layout.

b. Run your finger over all the letters to ensure the edges are adhered well.

c. Using a stamp pad, ink over the top of the letter stickers and the surrounding area. Work carefully so the results will look blended.

d. Coat the entire area with embossing powder, then shake off any excess powder.

e. Using a straight pin, carefully remove the letter stickers without getting embossing powder in the letter areas. Set the embossing powder with a heat gun.

Tips: Use die-cut, paper-backed letter stickers with the above techniques for the best results. Do not use this technique with plastic-backed letters, as heat guns will melt them. If too much embossing powder gets beneath a letter, use additional adhesive when placing the letter on a layout.

❸ **Stone look.** With this technique, you can change letter stickers of any color and use paint to make them look like stone (Figure 5). Just mix a tiny bit of black acrylic paint into white paint, taking care not to over mix it and destroy the mottled look. Next, apply the paint over the desired letter stickers. Let it dry, then pull the letter stickers carefully off the backing and place them on your layout.

④ Crimping. A quick way to add texture to letter stickers is to crimp them (Figure 6). Simply place the stickers on cardstock, adhering them firmly. Run the letter stickers through a crimper. To emphasize the crimping on my examples, I used my fingers to apply a dusting of chalk to the letters' top ridges.

⑤ Whitewash. Do you have letter stickers in a style you love but the color is too bright? Tone it down with the whitewash technique. Using a dry paintbrush or stipple brush, dip the brush into white paint or ink.

Dab the excess on a paper towel, then drag the brush across your letter stickers to apply the whitewash effect. The results will be more muted (Figure 7). Let the letter stickers dry, or set the paint with a heat gun before removing the stickers and adhering them to your layout.

⑥ Aging. Sometimes letter stickers are too shiny, too colorful, or too perfect. Here are a few ways to "age" your letters for a well-worn look. Be sure to cut the individual letter stickers away from their sheet first.

a. Sand. Use a fine-grade sandpaper to remove some of the color from the letter stickers and make them look more blended. This is a great way to use those camouflage or patterned letter stickers (Figure 8).

b. Fold. Fold your letter stickers to add texture. Make folds on the stickers one at a time. At each fold, rub or scratch the crease. In Figure 9, I applied metallic rub-ons to add color to the folds.

c. Crosshatch. Take a straight pin and scratch the letter stickers' surface horizontally and vertically, creating tiny crosses (see Figure

Figure 12. Save space on your page by placing letter-sticker titles and captions in your photo frame. *Title by Mary Larson.* **Supplies** *Letter stickers and cardstock:* SEI, Inc.

Figure 13. Use different shapes and bright colors to make your titles pop. *Title by Mary Larson.* **Supplies** *Letter stickers:* Mrs. Grossman's ("Grant, Wyatt, Kent, Kurt") and Paperfever ("My Sons"); *Square punch:* Family Treasures.

10). The scratches don't have to be perfect, and if the letter stickers tear a little, that's okay. You want a roughened look for your letters.

⑦ Punch and layer. For a new and easy twist, punch and layer any larger-sized letter sticker, solid or patterned. You'll need two different colors of letters with the same font.

First, place the color of letter you want for the background down on your layout. While the letter sticker in the second color is still on its backing, punch shapes.

Remove the second color letter sticker from its backing and place it on top of the first letter sticker. The bottom sticker letter's color will show through the punched-out areas. I used a rectangle punch for Figure 11, but a small flower, circle or square punch would also work well.

Placement Ideas

You're not limited to placing letter stickers across the top of your layout. Consider the following:

◆ Use clear-backed letter stickers on photographs (see foot photo in Figure 6) or for creative journaling highlights.

◆ Combine letters or punctuation to create decorative accents (see "Fingers & Toes" section in Figure 6).

◆ Use letter stickers in tight spaces such as photo frames (Figure 12).

◆ Create interesting titles by wrapping letter stickers inside circles, ovals and other shapes (Figure 13).

◆ Mix and match sizes and fonts for different looks. In Figure 2, I used different-colored letters and overlaid them with beads.

Now that you're savvier about what you can do with letter stickers, give these techniques a try. They're fun and fresh—just what you need to make your layouts look fabulous! ♥

Letter Sticker Companies

If you love the look of custom letters but lack the time or talent, relax.
The following companies manufacture letter stickers with custom, stylish looks:

◆ **Autumn Leaves**
www.autumnleaves.com

◆ **Beary Patch, Inc.**
www.bearypatchinc.com

◆ **Bo-Bunny Press**
www.bobunny.com

◆ **ChYOPs**
801/205-3268

◆ **Colorbök**
www.colorbok.com

◆ **Creative Imaginations**
www.cigift.com

◆ **D. J. Inkers**
www.djinkers.com

◆ **Frances Meyer**
www.francesmeyer.com

◆ **K & Company**
www.kandcompany.com

◆ **Karen Foster Design**
www.karenfosterdesign.com

◆ **Making Memories**
www.makingmemories.com

◆ **me & my BIG ideas**
www.meandmybigideas.com

◆ **Mrs. Grossman's**
www.mrsgrossmans.com

◆ **My Mind's Eye**
www.frame-ups.com

◆ **Paper Adventures**
www.paperadventures.com

◆ **Paper House Productions**
www.paperhouseproductions.com

◆ **Pioneer Photo Albums**
www.pioneerphotoalbums.com

◆ **Provo Craft**
www.provocraft.com

◆ **Sandylion Sticker Products**
www.sandylion.com

◆ **Scrap in a Snap**
www.scrapinasnap.com

◆ **SEI, Inc.**
www.sei.com

◆ **S.R.M. Press, Inc.**
www.srmpress.com

◆ **Stampendous!**
www.stampendous.com

◆ **Stickopotamus**
www.stickopotamus.com

◆ **The C-Thru Ruler Company**
www.cthruruler.com

◆ **Tie Me To The Moon**
www.tiemetothemoon.com

◆ **Westrim Crafts**
www.westrimcrafts.com

◆ **Wish in the Wind**
www.wishinthewind.com

D.J. Inkers

Mrs. Grossman's

Sonnets, Creative Imaginations

Stampendous

Bo-Bunny Press

Paper House
Productions

ChYOPs

Stickopotamus

Sandylion

Beary Patch

fabulous fibers

10 ways to fluff, wind, wrap, weave and braid them

Figure 1. Tassels make a fun frame element for your page. *Page by Mary Larson.* **Supplies** *Patterned paper:* Sonnets, Creative Imaginations; *Fibers:* Funky Fibers; Rubba Dub Dub, Art Sanctum; *Computer font:* CK Twilight, "Fresh Fonts" CD, *Creating Keepsakes; Metallic rub-ons:* Craf-T Products; *Rub-on transfers:* Impress-ons, Creative Imaginations; *Other:* Nailheads and brad.

Dress alikes?

Just by chance Grant and his Aunt Roanna wore the same outfit one day. She teased him like crazy about it! He was shy about it, but finally agreed to let me take their picture. It's a good thing; sometimes I forget to take pictures of my siblings with my children, a very important thing to do.

Aunt Roanna loves my kids as if they were her own. We always love spending time together. She'll even hunt bugs with them if they ask! Kind of a departure from the "norm" for her, since she only has daughters.

SWEATERS USED TO BE a staple in my wardrobe. Now that I live in Arizona, I rarely wear them. In fact, I own very few sweaters. I'm more interested in the "stuff" sweaters are made of—fibers!

When fibers came into the scrapbooking world, I was hooked. They add just the right touch to any layout. They're safe for your layouts, and they go with every style. Let's take a look at how to use them and experiment with a few new ideas.

BY MARY LARSON

Figure 2. Jazz up a traditional tassel with multicolored fibers. *Sample by Mary Larson.* **Supplies** *Fibers:* On the Surface; Rubba Dub Dub, Art Sanctum.

Figure 3. Dress up a plain tag with a touch of fiber. *Sample by Mary Larson.* **Supplies** *Fibers:* Fibers By The Yard; *Tag:* Avery; *Metal accent:* Scrapyard 329.

Figure 4. Add texture to die cuts and hand-cut accents by adhering fibers to them. *Sample by Mary Larson.* **Supplies** *Fibers:* Rubba Dub Dub, Art Sanctum.

Fluff It Up

Tassels are a natural when it comes to fiber accents. Like tags, they can be unique embellishments on your layouts. Here are a few variations:

Faux Medallion Tassel

❶ Take a square, circular or rectangular piece of cardstock and place double-stick tape along the perpendicular edges.
❷ Cut lengths of fiber and attach the ends along each taped edge. Use all one color and type or mix them up for a little variety.
❸ Adhere an identical cardstock shape over the fibers to sandwich them between the cardstock.
❹ Decorate the cardstock shape with a nailhead, button, punched shape, patterned paper, chalks or metallic rub-ons.
❺ Tie coordinating fibers around the hanging fibers. Trim off the ends or tuck them behind the other fibers (Figure 1).

Traditional Tassel

❶ Cut a piece of cardboard at least 2" wide by the desired length of your tassel. Wrap a piece of fiber around the length of the cardboard. The more you wrap, the thicker your tassel will be.
❷ Thread a coordinating fiber through the top loops, tie it tightly, then gently pull the fibers off the cardboard.
❸ Cut the bottom loops.
❹ Tie another strand of coordinating fiber around the tassel between ½" and 1" from the top.
❺ Fluff out the strands (Figure 2).

Tagged Tassel

Give a new twist to the traditional tag. Apply double-stick tape to the bottom edge of the tag. Lay fiber strands along the tape, and trim the strands if needed. Tie matching fibers through the tag hole. Turn the tag over and embellish it as desired (Figure 3).

Stick It Down

Create an accent by strategically positioning fibers on a neutral or coordinating piece of cardstock. Choose a simple design, such as a flower, flag or sun (Figures 4 and 5). Run the cardstock through a Xyron machine or apply an even coat of liquid glue. Start adhering the fibers to the adhesive. Trim off the excess cardstock when you are finished.

You can also cover a die cut or pre-formed shape with fibers.

Wrap It Around

Wrapping fibers around page elements is one of my favorite ideas. It's easy and makes a big impact. Try these creative ideas:

Wrap a Border

Tape a strand of fiber to the back of a strip of corrugated cardstock. Starting at the top, randomly wrap the fiber around the strip until you

Figure 5. Combine flat and fluffy elements to make a unique American flag accent. *Page by Mary Larson.* **Supplies** *Textured paper:* Hollander's; *Fibers:* Funky Fibers and Fibers By The Yard; *Computer font:* AmerTypeCnd, downloaded from the Internet; Impact, Microsoft Word; *Chalk:* Craf-T Products; *Nailheads:* Making Memories; *Brads:* American Tag Company; *Other:* Aluminum tag and star nailhead.

reach the bottom, then attach it to the back of the cardstock with tape. I like to wrap my borders with multiple strands of fibers (Figure 6).

For a more subtle look, wedge fiber strands into the ridges of the corrugated paper.

Wrap a Frame

Select a pre-printed photo frame or create your own. Tape one end of the fiber to the underside of the frame, then wrap it in and out of the frame's opening (Figure 7). Try wrapping photo corners, page corners, letters, tags and more!

Wind and Bind It

Using yarn and thread techniques you already know, create unique elements to add to your pages.

Braid It

Choose three different fibers and attach them to one end of your cardstock. Braid the fibers loosely (as shown in Figure 8) or tightly. Use glue dots or liquid glue to

Figure 6. Mix fiber colors and textures to add interest to a border. *Page by Mary Larson.* **Supplies** *Corrugated cardstock:* DMD Inc.; *Fibers:* Adornments, EK Success; Rubba Dub Dub, Art Sanctum; *Computer font:* Cricket, downloaded from the Internet; *Other:* Nailhead.

Figure 7. Customize a ready-made frame with fibers. *Sample by Mary Larson.* **Supplies** *Fibers*: Funky Fibers; *Frame*: Forget Me Not Designs; *Brads*: GoneScrappin.com

tack down the fibers along the way and at the finished end.

Crochet It

Use a loose crochet stitch to create a cool edge for your mats, borders or journaling blocks. This works best with solid color fibers that aren't too fluffy. That way, you can see the stitches (Figure 9).

Weave It

Secure three or more fibers vertically to your cardstock with tape. Place another three or more strands perpendicular to the first group. Weave the horizontal fibers over and under the vertical fibers (Figure 10). When the weaving is complete, secure all the edges.

Note: The more fibers you use, the more difficult this will be.

Other Uses

Don't forget these additional fun uses for fiber:
- Thread it through eyelets or holes.
- Tie it in bows or knots.
- Use it to outline letters, frames, borders and more.
- Embellish tags.
- Stitch page elements.

Fluffy, flat, sparkly, rough, soft, knobby, smooth, wide or narrow, fibers come in just about every texture imaginable. Colors are sometimes solid, sometimes variegated. At times, the fibers come with two, three or more colors combined. Some fibers come with two or more strands twisted together.

With a selection like this, you can always find the perfect fibers for your layouts. So, try a few of these ideas to fiber-up your pages! ♥

Figure 8. A loose braid of pretty fibers creates a lacy look. *Sample by Mary Larson.* **Supplies** *Fibers*: Funky Fibers; *Eyelets*: Making Memories.

Figure 9. A crochet stitch is a perfect use for beautiful fibers. *Sample by Mary Larson.* **Supplies** *Fibers*: Awesome Albums; *Eyelets*: Doodlebug Design; *Computer font*: Angelina, downloaded from the Internet.

Figure 10. Weaving is an easy way to show off colorful fibers. *Sample by Mary Larson.* **Supplies** *Fibers*: Making Memories; Rubba Dub Dub, Art Sanctum.

fun with
shape templates

Try these fresh approaches

Figure 1. Embossed frames highlight pictures in an elegant, easy way. *Page by Mary Larson.* **Supplies** *Square and rectangle templates:* Fiskars; *Patterned papers:* Sandylion and K & Company; *Ink pads:* Brilliance, Tsukineko; Adirondack, Ranger Industries; *Alphabet stamps:* PSX Design and Ma Vinci; *Screws and square tag rims:* Making Memories; *Rulers:* Limited Edition; *Metallic rub-ons:* Craf-T Products; *Embossing tool:* Empressor, Chatterbox; *Computer font:* CK Extra, "Fresh Fonts" CD, *Creating Keepsakes.*

IF YOU'VE SCRAPBOOKED for a while, you probably own a few shape templates. They're the sturdy guides designed to help you cut precise ovals, circles, stars, squares and custom shapes. And you probably think you've tapped their capabilities. Think again! I'll review basic tracing and cutting with a template, then share a few tricks that'll have you looking at your templates through new eyes.

Basic Instructions

If you've seen shape templates before but haven't used one, here's a quick how-to

BY MARY LARSON

Place your template over your photo to determine the best size. *Photo by Kathy Spann.*

Figure 2. Fun embellishments and bright fibers make a cute spring tag. *Example by Mary Larson.* **Supplies** *Circle template:* Westrim Crafts; *Fibers:* Rubba Dub Dub, Art Sanctum; *Leaves:* Black Ink; *Brads:* GoneScrappin.com; *Pebble:* Marcel Schurman Creations; *Other:* Charm.

that'll help you use templates with ease:

❶ Decide which shape template to use, then place it on a piece of paper or photograph.

❷ Affix the template to your paper or photograph with removable tape or a temporary adhesive to prevent slippage.

❸ With a pencil, trace lightly and slowly on the inside of the template. Stay close to the edge.

❹ Carefully remove the tape from your template and lift the paper or photograph.

❺ Cut just inside the pencil marks you've drawn on your paper or photograph.

Fun Techniques to Try

Once you've got the basics down, pull out your shape templates and give one or more of the following a try.

Embossed Frames

While dry embossing with a template isn't exactly new, you can combine more than one size or shape to create an interesting accent. Here's how to create the fun look in Figure 1:

❶ Select two different sizes of square or rectangle templates. Position the smallest shape on your cardstock, then affix the shape with removable tape or a temporary adhesive. Note: Do not tape inside the shape.

❷ Flip your template and cardstock (now attached) over. Rub the cardstock with wax paper to prepare it for embossing. (This will help the stylus move more smoothly.)

❸ With your finger, feel for the start of the shape and place your stylus there. Move it slowly yet firmly around the shape's outline

until you've made a deep impression. Repeat the process if needed. Note: Take care not to press so hard that you tear the cardstock.

❹ Lift the template off carefully. Position the larger shape evenly around the embossed smaller shape and affix as in step 1, then repeat steps 2–4.

❺ When you're finished, trim around the larger, outside shape, then use metallic rub-ons or chalk to emphasize the impressions. To create the mitered-look corners, I

Pull out your shape templates and put them to good use. You'll love the clever looks you can create!

Figure 3. Mix embossed shapes to create a clever accent. *Example by Mary Larson.* **Supplies** *Circle and square templates:* Provo Craft; *Patterned paper:* O'Scrap!, Imaginations; *Sticker:* Pressed Petals; *Metallic rub-ons:* Craf-T Products.

held a scrap piece of cardstock diagonally at the corners when I was applying the rub-ons.

Consider the following variations as well:

♦ Instead of using the raised side of the paper, use the recessed side (see the tag in Figure 2) to surround your embellishment.

♦ Use two different shapes (such as the square and circle in Figure 3).

Figure 4. Graphic letters, numbers and shapes help a layout "pop" visually. *Page by Mary Larson.* **Supplies** *Square template:* Fiskars; *Patterned papers:* Karen Foster Design and 7 Gypsies; *Computer font:* 2Peas Jack Frost, downloaded from *www.twopeasinabucket.com*; *Number stamp:* Ma Vinci; *Punches:* Family Treasures; *Pen:* Slick Writer, American Crafts.

Tracing

I know, tracing is what you usually do with templates. But did you know you can combine shape sizes and use a simple pen to create a graphic, eye-catching border? (See Figure 4.) Here's how:

❶ Find the middle of your border. (I started at the corner since I was making both a vertical and horizontal border.)

❷ Decide how wide you want the border shapes to be. Select a shape template that's similar in size, position it on your paper, and carefully trace inside the shape. Lift the template immediately.

❸ Before you place the template down again, wipe any wet ink off. Choose a shape template with either a larger or smaller shape and position it next to the first shape

you've drawn, overlapping the corners. *Tip:* When using squares or rectangles, make sure the overlapped lines are parallel and perpendicular to the template.

❹ Repeat step 3 until you've completed your border.

After I drew my squares, I punched black squares to place inside the larger drawn squares. Next, I punched smaller squares from patterned paper and placed those randomly over the black squares.

Outlining

Shape templates work well for drawing geometric shapes on scrapbook pages. Soften the look by gluing fibers over the outline after tracing. This works especially well with circles and ovals (see

Figures 5 and 6).

To create an outline with fiber:

❶ Choose a corresponding shape template. Tape it down on your paper, then apply liquid glue around the inside of the shape.

❷ Position fiber carefully over the adhesive, following the inside of the shape. Remove the template. *Tip:* Let the glue set up for a minute so the fiber will be easier to keep in place.

Filling

Use templates to create a filled shape (Figures 7 and 8). While the shape may not be perfect, a template will give you more control over placement and size. You can generally pick from multiple shape sizes on the same template, so it's easy to pick what you need for

Figure 5. Fashion an interesting border with fibers and circles. *Page by Mary Larson.* **Supplies** *Circle template:* Fiskars; *Patterned paper:* Creative Imaginations (Renae Lindgren line) and Magenta; *Brads:* GoneScrappin.com; *Fibers:* Rubba Dub Dub, Art Sanctum; *Metal corners:* Making Memories; *Computer fonts:* JanieHmk, Hallmark Card Studio, Sierra Home; CK Wanted, "Fresh Fonts" CD, *Creating Keepsakes.*

Figure 6. Highlight a special quote by encircling it with fibers. *Example by Mary Larson.* **Supplies** *Oval template:* The C-Thru Ruler Co.; *Computer font:* Cézanne, P22 Type Foundry; *Brads:* American Tag Company; *Chalk:* Craf-T Products; *Liquid glue:* Mono Multi Adhesive, Tombow; *Other:* Fiber and heart charm.

Answers to Common Questions

Interested in using shape templates but have a few questions? Here are answers to some of the most common questions.

Q. Can I crop a photograph using a template?

A. Yes, a template makes a good guide for cutting photographs. Just be sure to use a photo-safe pencil when tracing your shape.

Q. How do I determine which part of the photograph to crop off?

A. Decide if you want to center your subject or keep it off-center, then determine how much of the background you should cut out. Circles and ovals are good for removing distracting background elements and keeping the focus on the subject. Just watch your edges carefully to make sure you don't cut off something important.

Q. What kind of writing utensil should I use for tracing?

A. You can use either a sharp pencil or a fine-tip pen. When drawing shapes, experiment with different pen widths to find what will look best with your layout.

Q. I'm still having trouble with the template and paper slipping. What can I do?

A. If slippage is still a problem after you've taped the template to the paper, use a temporary adhesive to secure your paper to your work surface. This will help prevent slippage.

Q. What can I do to make cutting the shape easier?

A. Use sharp-tipped scissors for cutting. Move the paper instead of the scissors to get a smoother cut.

Q. How can I make a shaped photograph look good on my layout?

A. Mat the shaped photograph using the next bigger shape on your template. Keep your shaped photographs to a minimum. One or two ovals or circles are enough to emphasize the photographs without distracting from them.

Figure 7. Create a shimmery, lovely flower with glittery paint and mica chips. *Example by Mary Larson.* **Supplies** *Oval and circle templates:* EK Success; *Glitter paint:* Stickles; *Diamond sequins:* Diamondz, Suze Weinberg; *Mica flakes:* USArtQuest.

Figure 8. Customize a simple shape with products that'll make it extra special. *Example by Mary Larson.* **Supplies** *Rectangle template:* Provo Craft; *Glitter and shaved ice:* Magic Scraps; *Chalk:* Craf-T Products; *Ink pad:* Colorbox, Clearsnap; *Embossing powder:* Stamp-N-Stuff; *Beads:* Halcraft.

Shape Template Companies

Who makes shape templates? Several companies! Following is a quick sampling.

◆ **The C-Thru Ruler Co.**
www.cthruruler.com

◆ **Close To My Heart**
www.closetomyheart.com

◆ **Creative Memories**
www.creativememories.com

◆ **EK Success**
www.eksuccess.com

◆ **Fiskars**
www.fiskars.com

◆ **Frances Meyer**
www.francesmeyer.com

◆ **Provo Craft**
www.creativexpress.com

◆ **Puzzle Mates**
www.puzzlemates.com

◆ **Stampin' Up!**
www.stampinup.com

◆ **Westrim Crafts**
www.westrimcrafts.com

your page or embellishment.

Consider the following possibilities as well:
◆ Draw an item with a combination of shapes (Figure 7). With a little creativity, you can make almost anything! After tracing your shape, fill it in with 3-D paint or Stickles Glitter Glue. Let the design dry.
◆ Trace your shape, then fill it with a liquid adhesive. Sprinkle with glitter, shaved ice, beads or sequins. Tap off the excess and let the design dry.

◆ Hold the template firmly in place, then stroke chalk from the outside edges in.
◆ With the template firmly in place, apply ink with an ink pad. Dab inside the shape until it's completely covered. Add embossing powder and set with heat if desired.

Now that you've got fresh ideas, pull out those shape templates and put them to good use. You'll love the clever looks you can create! ❤

sticky stuff

How to choose—and use—adhesives well

UPON EXAMINING A HERMAFIX DISPENSER, my husband turned to me and asked, "What's this?"

"An adhesive," I said.

He held up a roll of Glue Dots. "These?"

"Adhesive."

"Then what are those?" He motioned toward pop dots, a bottle of glue, and some double-stick tape. After his inquisition was through, I had seven different adhesives in front of me—and they were just the ones from my tackle box of frequently used supplies.

It's difficult to explain the importance of variety to a man who looks into our closet and wonders why I have so many pairs of black shoes. He's content with four pairs. Total. But I believe you never know *what* you're going to need *when*, so it's better to be prepared!

Types of Adhesive

Selecting an adhesive is like finding favorite shoes: it's all based on what suits the occasion and what you're comfortable with. But first, you need to become familiar with the available styles. So, for those of you just starting out (or those who'd like a refresher), here's a quick summary:

◆ **Corners.** Photo corners come in two styles. You'll find double-sided adhesive triangles that sit beneath the photo. You'll also find the traditional type that "holds" the photo, keeping it untouched by adhesive. Manufacturers include 3L Corp., 3M, Canson, Kolo and Pioneer Photo Albums.

◆ **Dots.** Double-sided, pressure-sensitive Glue Dots have great strength to hold embellishments and more. For exact coverage, you can buy Sticky Dots in sheets, while Hermafix

Transfer dots roll out from a refillable dispenser. Manufacturers include Herma, Glue Dots International and Therm O Web.

◆ **Foam.** Add dimension with double-sided foam mounts in tape, dot or square form that "lift" items from the page. Manufacturers include 3M, All Night Media, Cut-It-Up, Making Memories, Ranger Industries, Rogers and Therm O Web.

◆ **Glue Stick.** Paste-type glue in a convenient applicator lets you add dabs just where you need them.

Manufacturers include 3M, Avery, Fiskars, Manco, New Product Inc., Pioneer Photo Albums, Rogers and Saunders.

ARTICLE BY DENISE PAULEY

◆ **Liquid Glue.** Available in bottles and pen form (where glue glides out like ink), glue forms a strong bond and allows you to apply even the smallest amount with precision. Manufacturers include Avery, Close To My Heart, Delta, Duncan Enterprises, EK Success, Fiskars, Lineco, Magic Scraps, Making Memories, Marvy Uchida

Sailor, Thermo O Web, Tombow and Yasutomo.

◆ **Sheets.** Apply a smooth, thin layer of adhesive manually with double-sided sheets. Or, choose a Xyron unit that applies strong adhesive to the back of an entire photo or accent with the turn of a handle. Manufacturers include Avery, Close To My Heart, Epson, Grafix, Magic Scraps, Saunders and Xyron.

◆ **Sprays.** Aerosol spray adhesive is a quick and easy way to adhere large accents and textured or sheer materials, such as fabric and vellum. Manufacturers include 3M, Creative Imaginations and Krylon.

◆ **Tabs.** Whether you choose a box of traditional mounting squares with removable backings or tabs in a roll-out dispenser, these double-sided squares are ideal for adhering photos. Manufacturers include 3L Corp., Canson, Century Craft, Hermafix, Lineco, Manco, Pioneer Photo Albums,

Therm O Web and Xyron.

◆ **Tape.** Available in dispensers and rolls, double-sided tape is perfect when you need a strong bond for heavier items or for holding pocket pages or full-page mats. Some brands are heat-resistant, so they can be heat embossed as well. Manufacturers include 3L Corp., 3M, Kokuyo USA, Lineco, Manco, Pioneer Photo Albums, Ranger Industries, Therm O Web and Tombow.

Sticky Situation: Is Your Adhesive Safe?

To keep your albums archivally safe, adhesives should be acid- and Xylene-free. In addition to being photo-safe, they should also be permanent to stand the test of time, keeping everything in place years from now. (Several adhesives that meet these criteria have been given the CK OK seal of approval.)

Some adhesives marketed to crafters (such as those by Elmer's) aren't acid free but produce cool, artistic effects. When considering these products (such as dimensional glues, glazes, varnishes or sealers for decoupage), weigh your desire for the decorative element against your need to have a page that's 100% archivally sound. The choice is up to you.

Sticky Situation: Permanent or Repositionable?

If you need to tack something down temporarily (to check placement or to hold a stencil to your page, for example), many manufacturers of tapes, sheets and dots offer repositionable versions of their most popular adhesives.

In addition, several liquid glues and glue sticks have both permanent and repositionable features.

For a permanent bond, apply glue, attach immediately, and press for a moment to set. For a temporary hold, apply glue lightly, then allow it to dry until tacky before placing.

Spray adhesives are often repositionable for up to five minutes, while Hermafix Transfer holds well, but can be removed later and wiped clean from most surfaces.

Sticky Situation: Glue Glitches

Adhesives offer the hold you need, but they can trip you up as well. Here's how to deal with the following glue glitches:

◆ **Items that need to be moved.** Even if you choose a permanent adhesive, you can still correct mistakes or remove items after they've bonded.

Whenever I'm placing an object that may need to be removed years from now (for whatever reason), I use photo tabs. Though they're permanent, they can still be taken up with little or no damage to your photo or page. Gently pry up a corner with a chiseler, then continue to lift the item carefully without bending. Any remaining tabs can be scraped from the page.

Glue, however, is not quite as forgiving. If you need to lift something that's solidly stuck, reach for the un-du. To remove a hand-cut

letter, for example, apply a generous amount until the letter is saturated (the letter will dry and can be reused). Use the bottle's attachment to lift the edge, then carefully chisel the letter from the page. If you used a lot of adhesive, you may need to apply more un-du directly to your page to remove any residual glue. You can also use un-du to help remove other stubborn adhesives.

◆ **Too much glue.** I tend to be a bit overzealous when using glue. It's common for me to press an accent on my page, then see glue seeping from the edges—leaving a sticky, glossy residue as it dries.

To remove excess dried glue, try a little un-du or a Glue Eraser or Adhesive Pick Up Square (these act like erasers, rubbing the excess from the page). Or, try using a photo tab! Simply press the tab on

the dried glue, rub, then peel back slowly (a pouncing motion works faster but can cause micro tears). These methods also remove excess Sticky Dots or Xyron residue.

Sticky Situation: Tricky Sticking

Textured objects, mixed media and delicate handmade paper add interest to a page, but they're not always easy to adhere. Here are a few options to help the most difficult ones stay where they're stuck:

◆ **Fibers.** Tame flyaway fibers by tacking them down in strategic spots with tiny dabs of liquid glue or mini glue dots (elongated by stretching to "hide" under fibers).

◆ **Crumpled cardstock.** Use generous swoops of liquid glue, a trip through the Xyron, or strips of double-sided tape to hold this excessively bumpy texture.

◆ **Metal.** Try liquid glue (hold for a second to prevent sliding), Glue Dots or double-sided tape to hold heavy metal accents.

◆ **Mesh.** Spray adhesive will do the trick on metal mesh or mesh paper without showing through. Hold

firmly until set.

◆ **Delicate paper.** Lacy fabrics and handmade paper can be adhered with spray adhesive. Some designs, however, feature solid spots that can hide glue dots.

◆ **Pressed flowers.** Dabs of liquid glue or sprays work best since both allow you to add adhesive without bending the delicate petals (Figure 1).

◆ **Small stuff.** When working with tiny punch pieces, sequins, mini buttons or the like, try Glue Dots or Sticky Dots for a quick hold. If the item is delicate, squeeze a small amount of glue onto scrap paper, then use a toothpick to apply it.

◆ **Ribbon.** Keep ribbon looking smooth and beautiful by tacking it down lightly with glue dots, Sticky Dots or snippets of double-sided tape.

HOLDING IN PLACE

Figure 1. When working with delicate paper, flowers and leaves, use spray adhesives or specks of liquid glue to keep items intact. *Example by Denise Pauley*. **Supplies** *Handmade paper:* ArtisticScrapper.com; *Textured cardstock:* Canson; *Pressed flowers:* Nature's Pressed; *Pen:* Zig Millennium, EK Success; *Tag:* DMD Inc.

Sticky Situation: Vellum

We love vellum's sheer, transparent beauty, but nothing ruins its lovely look more than warping or telltale spots of adhesive (Figure 2). Thank goodness you have options (in addition to using fasteners or overlapping another item where the vellum has been adhered) for attaching vellum without compromising its trademark qualities.

Some scrapbookers use the liquid glue/glue stick technique: they carefully apply and smooth a paper-thin layer of glue over the back of the entire piece. To be successful, you must work quickly, spread the glue evenly, and make sure it's light enough to avoid warping.

You can also use mounting squares and tape designed for vellum. You'll achieve the best results by applying the adhesive to the backing page (not the vellum itself), then pressing the vellum onto it gently.

A trip through the Xyron is a quick option to form a complete, secure hold. (Eliminate excess Xyron adhesive by running your fingernail around the edges of the object before removing the top sheet.) Spray adhesive will also help you adhere vellum while retaining its clear quality (Figure 3). Hold the can at least 12 inches from the vellum over a piece of scrap paper, then spray lightly to avoid puckering. (Despite what adhesive you choose, placing clear, light-colored vellum on dark paper may make it appear somewhat cloudy.)

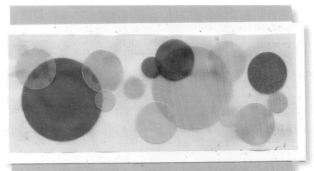

INCORRECT

Figure 2. Beware: Adhesive showing through can ruin vellum's lovely qualities. *Example by Denise Pauley.* **Supplies** *Vellum:* Paper Adventures and The Paper Company; *Circle punches:* EK Success and Marvy Uchida.

CORRECT

Figure 3. The correct techniques and adhesive choices keep vellum sheerly spectacular. *Example by Denise Pauley.* **Supplies** *Vellum:* Paper Adventures and The Paper Company; *Adhesives:* Creative Imaginations and Xyron.

Sticky Situation: Adhesive Additions

Think adhesives are only good for adhering? Think again! With a little experimentation, you can design cool, decorative elements for your pages. Here are a few ideas:

◆ **Paint.** Use a brush to "paint" designs with liquid glue. Allow the glue to dry until tacky, then sweep with Pearl-Ex, Perfect Pearls or chalk to add a touch of elegance (Figure 4).

◆ **Emboss.** Create a pattern with

Figure 4. Liquid glue can become the "paint" to bind pigment powder. *Example by Denise Pauley.* **Supplies** *Handmade paper:* ArtisticScrapper.com; *Textured cardstock:* Canson; *Wire word:* Making Memories; *Pigment powder:* Perfect Pearls, Ranger Industries.

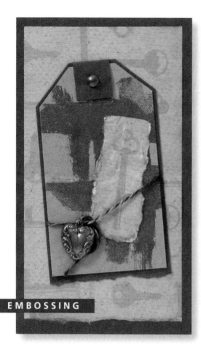

EMBOSSING

Figure 5. No ink? No problem. Use a glue stick to help you heat emboss! *Example by Denise Pauley.* **Supplies** *Patterned paper:* Design Originals; *Embossing powder:* Adirondack, Ranger Industries; *Fibers:* Making Memories; *Charm:* Boutique Trims; *Chalk:* Craf-T Products; *Stud:* Dritz.

heat-resistant double-sided tape and adhere to cardstock. Sprinkle second side with embossing powder and heat. (Use foam tape for a 3-D design.) You can also sweep a glue stick across an element to substitute for the ink before heat embossing (Figure 5).

◆ **Add glitz.** Use a tape dispenser to freehand swoops or letters, then sprinkle with seed beads to coat. Dress up a sticker or die cut by running the item face-down through a Xyron or pressing the item onto a sheet of Sticky Dots, then pushing firmly into a tray of clear seed beads. Position glue dots as centers of flowers, then add glitter or beads for sparkle.

◆ **Foil.** For a raised, heat-embossed look, freehand designs or paint over a stamped image with liquid glue. Allow to dry until tacky, rub a foil sheet over the top, then peel back gently.

◆ **Texturize.** To add texture to any element, apply a generous amount of glue stick. Use a brush or spatula

TEXTURIZING

Figure 6. Generous ridges of dried glue stick can create cool texture. *Example by Denise Pauley.* **Supplies** *Tag:* Forget Me Not Designs; *Alphabet stamps:* Limited Edition; *Stamping ink:* Tsukineko; *Pen:* Zig Writer, EK Success; *Metallic rub-ons:* Craf-T Products; *Craft wire:* Making Memories; *Charm:* Boutique Trims; *Bag:* DMD Inc.

to create ridges, then allow the glue to dry. Brush it with chalk, pigment powder or metallic rub-ons (Figure 6). ♥

Where to Find Adhesives

Here's a sampling of manufacturers:

3L Corp. *www.3lcorp.com*
3M. *www.3m.com*
Adhesive Technologies . . . . *www.adhesivetech.com*
Avery. . . . . *www.avery.com*
Close To My Heart. . . . . *www.closetomyheart.com*
Creative Imaginations . . . . *www.cigift.com*
Drytac . . . . *www.drytac.com*
Duncan Enterprises. . . . . *www.duncancrafts.com*
EK Success . . . . *www.eksuccess.com*
Elmer's. . . . . *www.elmers.com*
Fiskars . . . . *www.fiskars.com*
Glue Dots International. . . . . *www.gluedots.com*
Grafix. . . . . *www.grafixarts.com*

Herma. . . . . *www.herma.de*
Krylon . . . . *www.krylon.com*
Lineco . . . . *www.lineco.com*
Magic Scraps . . . . *www.magicscraps.com*
Making Memories. . . . . *www.makingmemories.com*
Manco . . . . *www.duckproducts.com*
Marvy Uchida . . . . *www.uchida.com*
Pioneer Photo Albums . . . . *www.pioneerphotoalbums.com*
Provo Craft . . . . *www.provocraft.com*
Rogers . . . . *www.rogerscorporation.com*
Sailor. . . . . *www.sailorpen.com*
Saunders. *www.saunders-usa.com*
Stampin' Up! . . . . *www.stampinup.com*
Therm O Web. . . . . *www.thermoweb.com*
Tombow . . . . *www.tombowusa.com*
un-du Products, Inc . . . . *www.un-du.com*
USArtQuest. *www.usartquest.com*
Xyron. . . . . *www.xyron.com*
Yasutomo. . . . . *www.yasutomo.com*

Available in white and blue, the Tombow Glue Stick won't warp, wrinkle or show through vellum.

Check out the handy adhesive applicators by Xyron.

50 ways to save big

Stretch your scrapbooking dollar

When I bought my first scrapbooking supplies a few years ago, choices were limited and I spent less than $20. Now, with an amazing array of products available, I can spend $20 before I've drawn my first breath of scrapbook store oxygen. Not only do I have poor shopping restraint, but the Allison method of fiscal responsibility dictates that any amount of money saved becomes immediate fodder for future spending.

Powered by that kind of incentive, I'm always looking for ways to save money. If you've got red blood in your veins, chances are you're a bargain shopper, too. Read on for 50 fantastic tips to help stretch your scrapbooking dollar.

by Allison Strine

save big

7

Paint chips, especially the metallic samples, make great accents.

Pages by Marissa Perez.
Supplies *Computer font:* Times New Roman, Microsoft Word; *Square punch:* EK Success; *Other:* Paint chips, foam tape and pen.

Prudent Purchasing

1 Shop prepared. To avoid purchasing duplicate products, keep a supply inventory notebook in your purse. Keep a list of your scissors, favorite papers and templates. Glue a sample from each punch you own on a page. On another page, draw a line from each of the pens you own.

2 Certain products, like cardstock, are less expensive when you buy in bulk. Split the paper and the cost with a friend.

3 If your local scrapbook store has a stocked crop room, you can use its die-cut machines, stencils, punches and more for a small fee.

4 Some products seem expensive at first glance, but with a second look you can use them in ways that actually save money. For instance, certain metal-rimmed tags have two useable sides, offering you the choice of using one side, the other or both. You can also separate the tags from the metal rims, creating three elements from one product.

5 Buy unmounted stamps—they can be up to half off the retail price. (An unmounted stamp refers to the rubber die only, without the cushion and mounting block.)

6 Make your own light box with a glass table and a light bulb. (A glass casserole dish works if you don't have a glass table.) Remove the shade and place the lamp under the table.

7 Paint chips, especially the metallic samples, make great accents. And the price is right—free! They come in a huge variety of colors. You might even motivate yourself to repaint your scrapbook area.

8 Watch for the discount coupons and ads in the Sunday newspaper. Craft stores frequently advertise super sales and print coupons. Many scrapbook stores also have weekly and monthly specials. Be sure to sign up for store mailers.

4

Certain metal-rimmed tags have two useable sides.

Supplies *Rubber stamps:* Junque (tags) and Cat's Life Press (writing); *Stamping ink:* Clearsnap and Ranger Industries; *Paints:* Lumiere, Jacquard Products; *Other:* Thread and fabric.

9 Browse your local dollar store for surprising treasures. Look for page accents, supplies and project ideas.

10 Use what you have. If you don't have the right shade of blue cardstock, create the shade instead of buying it. You'll surprise yourself with your resourcefulness.

11 This may shock you, but you *don't* need every single supply on the market. Focus on one embellishment for a while. When you concentrate on one type of product, it's easier to avoid buying things that you may never use anyway.

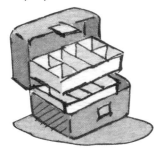

Economic Organization

12 Transparent or translucent film canisters are well suited for storing tiny scrapbook supplies like eyelets, buttons and beads.

13 Store your 12" x 12" paper in a pizza box. (It's often free if you ask a manager or employee at a local pizza parlor.) Take along a 12" x 12" piece of cardstock to make sure it fits.

14 Have a fisherman in the house? A tackle box is an affordable storage device for punches and small things. When opened,

the drawers are staggered so you can see everything at once.

15 For unmounted stamp storage, try CD jewel cases. The dies fit in the cases, and you can store the stamps by theme.

16 After you potty train your little one, turn your diaper bag into a portable supply storage case.

17 Recycle shipping boxes by turning them into magazine holders. Use a real holder as a template to draw lines on the box. Cut with a craft knife, then decorate.

Scrap and Scrimp

18 Share supplies like scissors, punches and embossing tools with a friend. Rummage through each other's cardstock and sticker stash;

you may use items the other can't bear to get rid of.

19 When your markers start running out, revive them by pouring a few drops of water into the ink cartridges.

20 Create your own stencils with heavy acetate. Print a computer design or draw one, then use a craft knife to cut it out.

21 S.O.S. stands for Save Our Scraps. Store paper scraps in hanging file folders or accordion files. Sort by color, then use the scraps for mats, paper piecings, shaker box contents and more. Make a cool background by grabbing a handful of one color and stitching the papers together in a crazy quilt.

12 Translucent film canisters work well for storing tiny scrapbook supplies.

Save big

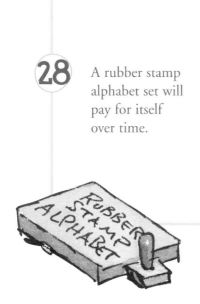

28 A rubber stamp alphabet set will pay for itself over time.

Supplies *Patterned paper and stickers:* Karen Foster Design; *Rubber stamps for title:* Wordsworth; *Stamping ink:* ColorBox, Clearsnap; *Computer fonts:* CK Corral, "Fresh Fonts" CD, *Creating Keepsakes*; Doodle Cursive, downloaded from the Internet.

22 Cosmetic sponges are useful for more than just makeup; use them to apply chalks and inks. Make cool background designs with a cosmetic sponge and ink.

23 Use a pair of decorative scissors as an alternative to a corner rounder. Some patterns are great for making cool corners. If you feel daring, try toenail clippers!

24 Remove buttons and a section of fabric from a treasured baby outfit and use them on a layout. Or, live dangerously and use the extra buttons that come with new clothing.

25 Cut square punches into triangles for quick photo corners.

26 Use paper strips instead of an entire sheet of cardstock to make a border.

27 Cut out the center of a photo mat or background paper and save the scrap for another project.

It Pays to Save Your Words

28 Invest in a rubber stamp alphabet set. It will pay for itself over time.

29 Sometimes, instead of stickers or die-cut letters, create a title by hand, using a good old-fashioned pen or marker.

30 After the initial investment, alphabet punches can save you a lot of money. You'll always have letters that coordinate perfectly, *and* you'll never worry about running out of an "A" just when you need one.

31 Download free fonts from the Internet. Go to *www.creatingkeep-sakes.com/magazine/backissues* and click on "January 2003," then "Font Frenzy," to view 25 web sites that offer free fonts and instructions for downloading.

Photo by Tamara Smith

27 Save scraps for another project.

38

Use plastic photo albums for storing die cuts and stickers.

Supplies *Stamping ink:* Fluid Chalk, ColorBox, Clearsnap; *Rubble, fibers and mesh:* Magic Scraps; *Text beads:* Stampers Anonymous; *Photo corners:* Canson; *Other:* Sticks, thread and flower.

32 Put your scraps to good use—print journaling on them. First, print your journaling on plain paper. Using temporary adhesive, stick your scrap over the journaling. Feed the paper through the printer again.

33 Use lettering templates. A small investment can save you a lot of money in the long run.

Photography Frugality

34 I *know* it's convenient, but one-hour photo developers are expensive. Instead, go to warehouse stores for normal photo developing. Remember, save money in one place and you get to spend it somewhere else!

35 Cotton make-up balls are an inexpensive way to remove fingerprints from photographs.

36 If you think you'll need reprints, get doubles. Not only is it less expensive in the long run, you may find creative freedom

knowing that if you wreck one photo you still have another.

37 For reprints and duplicate projects, scan photos into your computer and print them out. You can place several shots on one piece of photo paper, and of course you can resize and recolor the photographs.

38 If your photos come back in a plastic album, use it for storing die cuts and stickers. Separate them by theme.

Resourceful Penny Savers

39 Did you know your kitchen is a scrapbook haven? Cookie cutters are ideal for creating die cuts. Bowls and cups make great circle templates.

40 Your local school may have a die-cut machine available to the public. Go in with a smile and your own acid-free paper.

41 Check out back issues of scrapbook magazines from the

library. Try the crafts section of a discount or used bookstore.

42 Save brochures, tickets and souvenirs from vacations. Spray them with deacidification spray to protect them.

43 Make templates and die cuts with plastic lids from coffee cans.

44 Nature provides great page accents. Consider using leaves and dried flowers on your scrapbook pages.

44

Nature provides great page accents.

save big

If you use every one of these tips, the exact savings is $412.57!

45 Don't know what to do with Christmas cards? Use portions as accents or create collaged backgrounds in holiday layouts.

46 Before you discard a clogged rolling ball glue pen, drip some un-du Adhesive Remover into the well under the tip of the pen. Soak it for a few seconds. You'll have a glue pen that functions like new.

47 To avoid wasting adhesive paper in your Xyron machine, run strips of scrap cardstock through it whenever there's a space to fill. Store the scraps and use them for punchies later.

48 Remember the old adage "One woman's trash is another's treasure"? Take a long look at your stash of supplies. Use an online auction site to cash in on your unwanted supplies. Many scrapbooking web sites have auction or "for sale or trade" sections. You can also post product requests.

Here are a few sites to get you started:

Ebay.com
Scrapvillage.com
Jangle.com
Scrapsahoy.com

49 Raid your child's craft supplies. After all, you bought them, right? For instance, craft foam is great for accents or shaker box filler. Kids' coloring books are a cool source of templates and clip art. Simply trace the images onto cardstock, scan them into your computer, or copy them onto transparencies.

50 Swap it! Online swaps are a great way to trade your extra supplies for someone else's. A hostess chooses the number of participants and picks a specific theme, such as baby stickers. Everyone sends items to the hostess, who divides the supplies among participants and mails the items out. (It's a nice gesture to send the hostess a little extra "something" for her work.)

There you have it. Using my $2.98 calculator, I've figured that if you use every one of these tips, the exact savings is $412.57. Using Allison logic, you are now duty bound to spend at least that much on scrapbook supplies. That's a lot of money, girls. Now get out there and start shopping! ❤

tag, tissue and transfer paper ideas

Figure 1. Place a large sticker across multiple small tags to create beautiful custom accents for your layout. *Page by Helen McCain.* **Supplies** *Stickers:* EK Success; *Tags:* The Paper Cut; *Letter stickers:* Mrs. Grossman's (green) and Creative Imaginations (black); *Word stickers:* Bo-Bunny Press; *Patterned paper and paper fasteners:* Chatterbox; *Date stamp:* Making Memories; *Mesh:* Maruyama, Magenta.

Using Large Stickers

I loved the strong, vibrant colors of an oversized flower-basket sticker and wanted to use it on a summer layout. I did not, however, want to lose the focus on my photos. To break up the colors and design, I stretched the sticker over three tags. Here's how:

❶ Remove the string and hole reinforcers from three manila tags.

❷ Place the tags side by side on a flat surface, making sure they're evenly lined up.

❸ Adhere the sticker to the tags and trim the excess sticker pieces. Use an X-acto knife to separate the tags. Mat each tag and replace the hole reinforcers. Add fiber and a large eyelet to each tag.

—*Helen McCain, Sun Prairie, WI*

ARTICLE BY LORI FAIRBANKS

Layered Tissue Frame

Tissue paper's translucence adds an interesting texture, and now manufacturers are making it especially for scrapbooks! To create the frame on my page (Figure 2), I cut a frame from chipboard, then covered it with several layers of tissue using a decoupage medium. The decoupage medium enhances the translucence of the tissue and allows the printed pattern to show through all layers. This technique is very easy and yields great results. Just follow these steps:

❶ Cut a frame from chipboard (or use a premade mat board frame). Tear tissue paper into pieces. The smaller the pieces, the more they will overlap, increasing the amount of pattern that will show through the decoupage.

❷ Brush the adhesive onto a small area on the frame. Lay a piece of tissue over the adhesive with extra extending beyond the frame. Don't worry about wrinkles! They add to the character of the frame. Lightly brush the piece of tissue with a thin layer of adhesive. Continue this process until you've covered the frame with two or three layers of tissue.

Tip: When you add the last layer, you may want to position pieces of tissue so that a certain pattern or word is showing.

❸ After the final layer, allow the frame to air dry, then brush it with an additional coat of decoupage medium. Use it to glue the raw edges of the extended tissue to the back of the frame, leaving the frame with finished edges.

Tip: If your frame starts to warp from the moisture of the adhesive, heat the frame with a heat gun and reshape it while it's warm. You can also use a heat gun to speed up the drying process, but be careful not to let the frame get too hot or the adhesive will bubble.

Variation: Mix metallic pigment powders in your decoupage medium to add a sparkle to your frame.

—*Tricia Rubens, Castle Rock, CO*

→

Figure 2. Create a beautiful vintage frame by decoupaging patterned tissue paper on a wide photo mat. *Page by Tricia Rubens.* **Supplies** *Patterned paper:* Design Originals (vintage images), DMD Inc. and K & Company (background script); *Mesh:* Maruyama, Magenta; *Patterned tissue paper for frame:* 7 Gypsies; *Stickers, metal frame and tags:* K & Company; *Ribbon charm, heart eyelet and metal phrase:* Making Memories; *Fabric labels:* me & my BIG ideas; *Brads:* Creative Imaginations; *Label holder:* Li'l Davis Designs; *Stamping ink and chalk:* Stampin' Up!; *Computer fonts:* 1942 Report and Hannibal Lecter, downloaded from the Internet; CK Newsprint, "Fresh Fonts" CD, *Creating Keepsakes; Other:* Buttons, hat pins and clothing tag.

New Slide Looks

Accentuate small photos or text blocks in a fun way by using slides as mini frames. Customize the frames by stamping them with a solvent-based ink like StazOn, wrapping them with fibers, or placing printed or stamped transparencies inside them to mimic actual slides!

Here are some cool slide looks to consider:

◆ Sprinkle metal leaf (or Shaved Ice by Magic Scraps) between two transparencies to add sparkle and texture to your slides.

◆ Cover the face of a slide with any adhesive-backed paper. Use the slide as your guide and cut away the excess paper with an X-acto knife.

—Emily Adams, Magic Scraps

Figure 3. Create unique page titles or photo captions by placing printed transparencies inside slide frames. *Samples by Emily Adams for Magic Scraps.* **Supplies** *Slide holders, printed transparency, denim and metallic sticker paper and metal leaf flakes:* Magic Scraps.

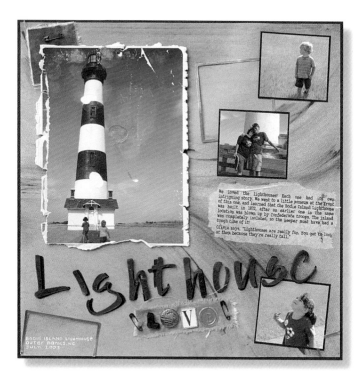

Print on Transfer Paper

I adore transferring visuals to polymer clay, but I'm not thrilled about using copy machine toner images. That's why I was excited to find a simple technique using inkjet prints and T-shirt transfer paper by Dottie McMillan at *www.polymerclaycentral.com*. Here's how to do the transfer:

❶ Print your picture onto T-shirt transfer paper. *Tip:* For a colorful result, use image-editing software to increase the saturation level (the amount of color) before you print.

❷ Prepare your clay by rolling it flat or running it through a pasta machine dedicated for clay use.

❸ Place the picture on the clay and burnish well. Don't miss any area or it won't transfer!

❹ Bake the clay in a preheated oven for about six minutes. Carefully remove the paper, then finish baking the clay for the manufacturer's recommended time.

—Allison Strine, Roswell, GA

Figure 4. Transfer an image to polymer clay with T-shirt transfer paper. *Page by Allison Strine.* **Supplies** *Patterned paper:* Teri Martin, Creative Imaginations; *Polymer clay:* Prēmo!, Sculpey; *Metal squares:* Sonnets, Creative Imaginations, *Title template:* Wordsworth, *Stamping ink:* ColorBox, Clearsnap, *Letter "V":* FoofaLa, *Safety pins:* Li'l Davis Designs, *Metal accent for letter "O":* Magic Scraps; *Craft paint:* Lumiere, Jacquard Products, *Computer font:* CK Corral, "Fresh Fonts" CD, *Creating Keepsakes; Other:* Fabric and tissue.

Photo Manipulation

My best friend, Dan, took this fantastic shot at our local beach. With his permission, I took liberties with the photograph to come up with this layout.

To create the look shown here, I used Microsoft Digital Image Pro to make two copies of Dan's photo. I took the first one and converted the photo to "chalk drawing." I put the other photo on top of the first one and used the eraser tool to erase some of the picture (to show the drawing behind it). I then combined both photographs and used "soft edge" manipulation to slightly blend the finished photograph into the background.

—Sheila McIntosh Dixon, Milton, FL

Figure 5. Use creative computer techniques to create unusual yet beautiful effects on your scrapbook pages. *Page by Sheila McIntosh Dixon.* **Supplies** *Computer program:* Microsoft Image Pro.

homemade stamps and more

Figure 1. Create your own stamps with cork. *Page by Jenni Bowlin.* **Supplies** *Metal watch-face stickers, bookplate, epoxy letters and metal stencil letter:* Li'l Davis Designs; *Patterned paper:* K & Company; *Ribbon and postcard:* me & my BIG ideas; *Letter stamps:* Rubber Stampede (large) and PSX Design (small); *Number and swirl stamps:* Postmodern Design; *Waxed fibers:* Waxy Flax, Scrapworks; *Mini brads:* American Tag Company; *Acrylic paint:* Delta Technical Coatings; *Other:* Cork stamp.

Cork Stamps

I love experimenting with anything that adds interesting texture to my pages, especially textures that produce a not-so-perfect finish. This quest led me to the discovery of stamping with cork. When used with acrylic paint, the cork's uneven pattern creates a finish similar to a sea sponge (see Figure 1). Unlike a sponge, cork is easy to cut into shapes. Here are a few pointers: →

ARTICLE BY LORI FAIRBANKS AND RACHEL THOMAE

Cork Stamps, Step by Step

① Trace your image onto the cork, then cut it out with a craft knife.

② Insert a pushpin into the center of your shape. This becomes your handle.

③ Coat the shape with an even layer of acrylic paint, then stamp the cork onto your desired surface. Apply pressure to all parts of the image with your fingers. Lift the stamp and repeat as desired.

Cork Pointers

♦ Look for cork tiles that are at least ¼" thick. You can usually find them at major discount and office supply stores.

♦ Stick to large, basic shapes. Diamonds, circles and flower petals are my favorites.

♦ Make sure your craft knife is very sharp; otherwise, your cork will crumble when you cut it.

Follow the steps at left to create your own cork stamps.

—*Jenni Bowlin, Mt. Juliet, TN*

Editor's Note: For other cool ideas with cork, see "Customized Cork" on page 172 in this issue.

Inking Letter Stamps

I used to stress when using mini letter stamps because I always got extra ink from the stamps' edges on my layout. Then I started using markers to ink my stamps. I apply the ink to just the letter part of the stamp. No more messy edges!

—*Candi Gershon, Fishers, IN*

HELP WITH HAND STITCHING

I like to do hand stitching on my layouts, but it can be tricky getting evenly spaced stitches. To address this, I lightly pencil in where I want to stitch. Next, I run the paper through my empty sewing machine (no bobbin or thread), making sure to follow my pencil line carefully. The result? Perfectly spaced holes that can now be easily stitched through. The whole thing takes a minute or two, compared to the untold time it takes to poke the holes by hand.

—*Jennifer Bates, Portland, OR*

Figure 2. Create lightweight mosaic tiles with acid-free cardboard. *Pages by Lisa Russo.* **Supplies** *Computer font:* Corona Light, downloaded from the Internet; *Patterned paper and cardboard tile:* Magenta; *Watercolor paints:* Angora; *Acrylic medium:* Liquitex; *Brads:* Memory Lane; *Letter stamps:* PSX Design and Hero Arts (small letters), Missing Link Stamp Co. (title letters) and OfficeMax (date); *Stamping ink:* ColorBox, Clearsnap; VersaMark, Tsukineko; *Embossing enamel:* Suze Weinberg; *Bookplate:* Two Peas in a Bucket; *Ribbon:* C.M. Offray & Son.

Faux Mosaic Tiles

Love those mosaic tiles that are all the rage? If you haven't been able to find them in the right color or you think the glass ones are too heavy, make your own from cardboard and craft supplies. I made faux mosaic tiles for my title in Figure 2. Just follow these easy steps:

❶ Using a brush or sponge, coat cardboard squares with Gesso, a white acrylic medium. Let them dry. (The Gesso seals and prepares your surface.)

❷ Paint over the Gesso with watercolors or acrylics, or sponge each surface with dye-based stamping ink. Allow the tiles to dry.

❸ Stamp your title letters using black pigment ink. Let them dry or emboss them with clear embossing powder.

(I embossed the tiles on my page.)

❹ Cover the squares with clear embossing ink, then coat them with a few layers of clear embossing powder. You can also coat each tile with a paper glaze, such as Crystal Lacquer or Diamond Glaze.

I sanded my tiles around the edges and sponged them with brown ink to help them fit my layout better. These tiles also look great as artistic borders, decorative photo mats, or page accents.

Variations: Try stamping images instead of letters, or simply paint the tiles and use them as page accents. Get another fun look by stamping directly on the Gesso finish.

—Lisa Russo, Carmel, IN

Figure 3. Use white embossing powder to add an icy touch to winter pages. *Page and samples by Christine Brown.* **Supplies** *Patterned papers:* PSX Design (blue) and Karen Foster Design (purple); *Computer fonts:* Adine Kinberg ("Belle") and Runic MT ("de l'Hiver"), downloaded from the Internet; 2Peas Chestnuts (journaling), downloaded from *www.two-peasinabucket.com;* *Stickers:* Jolee's for You, Sticko by EK Success; *Embossing ink:* VersaMark, Tsukineko; *Embossing powder:* PSX Design; *Tags:* Making Memories; *Mesh:* Magenta; *Other:* Ribbon.

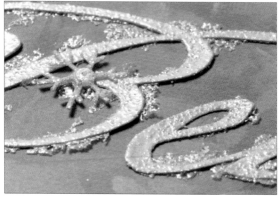

Snowy Title

I have a simple technique that can help you add a frosty, life-like touch of "snow" to your layouts. (See Figure 3.) You'll need a strong adhesive (a Xyron machine works well), clear embossing ink, and white or iridescent embossing powder (such as "Bridal" by PSX Design). Follow the easy steps shown at right.

❶ Run your title letters through a Xyron machine. Remove the clear plastic film. If you use a different adhesive, apply it to the back of your letters and place them, sticky side down, on a non-stick surface such as waxed paper.

❷ Coat the letters and surrounding area with embossing ink. Sprinkle the entire surface with embossing powder and heat.

❸ Gently lift the letters off the Xyron backing (or non-stick surface). As you lift, the feathery embossed area surrounding the letter will also lift off the backing, giving you a "snowy" look! Remove excess "snow" for a more natural look. The tip of a craft knife works well for getting into tight spots.

Variation: Use this technique to add a wintry look to snowflake punches, circle-punched snowmen, journaling blocks and photo mat edges.

—*Christine Brown, Hanover, MN*

Figure 4. Layer different colors of cardstock before die cutting your letters. *Page by Gillian Nelson.* **Supplies** *Die-cut letters:* Sophia, QuickKutz; *Computer font:* Newsprint, "Fresh Fonts" CD, *Creating Keepsakes.*

Vivid Title

To create the title in Figure 4, I layered different colors of cardstock, then used a QuickKutz die to make an impression of the letters. I had to hand cut the letters because the layers were too thick for the die cut. Still, the dies made a perfect imprint that I could use as a guide.

—*Gillian Nelson, Peoria, AZ*

Setting Tiny Eyelets

Try as I might, I never could set ⅟₁₆" eyelets with an eyelet setter. I'd either split the eyelet unevenly, or when I hammered the setter, it would slip and dent my paper.

I found that a Phillips screwdriver used for tightening eyeglasses fits perfectly. The cross of the screwdriver head splits the sides just right. I use a hammer to gently flatten the edges.

—*Rikki Garrett, Coweta, OK*

Tips & Tricks

Tag Tricks

Stretch your scrapbooking dollar with tags that have two separable metal rims, such as the Sonnets and Renae Lindgren tags by Creative Imaginations. Customize the extra tag with your own patterned paper, cardstock or vellum, or use the metal rim as a photo frame, journaling block or even an embellishment (Figures 5–7).

To separate the rims, carefully insert the tip of a craft knife blade between the tag's two rims. Gently twist the knife to separate the rims. Insert the blade multiple times around the perimeter of the tag. Cut the pre-attached string so you can completely remove the rim from the original tag.

—*Kristi Wright, Creative Imaginations*

Figure 5. Sharon wrapped the second tag rim with beaded wire to create a lovely embellishment. *Page by Sharon Soneff for Creative Imaginations.* **Supplies** *Patterned paper and metal-rimmed tags:* Sonnets, Creative Imaginations; *Craft wire:* Darice; *Brads:* Magic Scraps; *Brad rub-ons:* Bradwear, Creative Imaginations; *Beads:* Little Charmers.

Figure 6. Remove the back rim from a vellum tag and adhere a photo underneath the vellum. Use metal glue or mini glue dots to reattach the rim. *Tag by Sharon Soneff.* **Supplies** *Metal-rimmed vellum tag and poemstone:* Sonnets, Creative Imaginations. *Other:* Fiber and leaf bead.

Figure 7. Use the front rim "as is" and customize the back rim with a photo or journaling. *Tag by Kristi Wright.* **Supplies** *Metal-rimmed tag:* Renae Lindgren, Creative Imaginations; *Brads and brad rub-ons:* Bradwear, Creative Imaginations; *Letter stickers:* Shotz, Creative Imaginations; *Fibers:* Adornaments, EK Success.

custom labels and metal accents

Figure 1. Use stamping ink to enhance embossed cardstock. *Page and samples by Tracie Smith.* **Supplies** *Embossed cardstock:* K & Company; *Stamping ink:* Brilliance, Tsukineko (black); Stampin' Up! (green); Fluid Chalk, Clearsnap (blue); Ranger Industries (plum); *Ribbon:* Stampin' Up!; *Bubble type and frames:* Li'l Davis Designs; *Date stamp, square metal letters and metal word:* Making Memories; *Acrylic paint:* Delta Technical Coatings; *Pen:* Zig Millennium, EK Success; *Colored pencils:* Prismacolor, Sanford; *Concho:* Scrapworks; *Buckle:* Diane's; *Modeling paste:* Liquitex; *Watercolor paper:* Canson; *Other:* Chipboard and cardboard.

Inking Embossed Paper

Rub an inkpad over embossed cardstock to make the designs pop or to alter the paper to better match your layout. This direct-to-paper technique uses a few inkpads and some embossed cardstock.

Hold the inkpad in the palm of your hand and rub it gently over your embossed paper. Use light pressure to color only the raised images, or apply more pressure to change the color of the entire sheet of paper. Here are some fun variations:

- Use multiple shades of one color. For the layout in Figure 1, I used three different shades of blue for a blended look.

- Make your paper look more like fabric by rubbing the inkpad's edges over the background both vertically and horizontally.
- Use a chalk inkpad to create a soft, subtle look. Or, use a VersaMark pad to darken the inked areas like a watermark.
- Dress up the design with metallic inkpads.
- Use light-colored chalk inks or pigment inks on dark paper for dramatic results.

Experiment with your favorite designs and colors—I think you'll like what you end up with!

—*Tracie Smith, Smithtown, NY*

ARTICLE BY LORI FAIRBANKS

Creating Custom Labels

I love the look of Dymo labels on my layouts, but my muted color palettes tend to clash with standard label tape colors. On a whim, I ran a strip of patterned paper through my label maker and was delighted to discover that the imprinting worked! I tried vellum and thin metal next; it worked on these mediums as well. Here are a few tips for creating labels (see Figures 2–4):

◆ **Patterned paper or cardstock.**

(White-cored cardstock like that from Close To My Heart or Making Memories works best. Use darker colors for more contrast.)

❶ Cut paper strips small enough to fit your label maker. The width may vary, but it's usually slightly more than ¼".

❷ Feed a strip into the label maker. Push the strip all the way through until you can grab the other end.

❸ Test a few letters on a scrap strip. When using thicker paper, you may need to pull the strip to help it advance. Once you get the hang of it, punch out your words.

❹ Lightly sand the letters to remove the top layer of the paper and reveal the white core.

◆ **Vellum.**

(Use a heavier-weight vellum so the label maker doesn't punch all the way through it.)

❶ Cut the vellum into strips and feed them through the label maker as described above.

❷ Punch your words.

❸ Highlight the raised letters with chalk, metallic rub-ons, stamping ink or paint.

◆ **Thin metal.**

❶ Cut the thin metal into strips and feed them through the label maker as described above.

❷ Punch your words.

❸ If you used colored metal, lightly sand the letters to reveal the base color. If you used a pure metal, highlight the raised letters with a solvent ink such as StazOn by Tsukineko.

◆ **A few additional tips:**

◆ Label makers come in several fonts and sizes. Mixing and matching creates a fun look.

◆ Create a random look by pulling the strip in the label maker slightly to one side and then moving it back. This will cause the letters to punch unevenly.

◆ If you make a mistake while using patterned paper or metal, you may be able to pull the strip back into the label maker and re-punch it. The pressure smoothes out the previous letter, and you can then punch the correct letter in its place.

*—Heather Uppencamp,
Provo, UT*

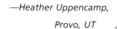

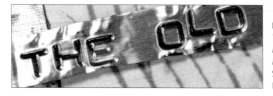

Figure 2. Thin strips of metal can be used with your Dymo label maker. *Tag by Heather Uppencamp.* **Supplies** *Patterned paper:* Anna Griffin; *Patterned vellum:* The Sharon Ann Collection, The C-Thru Ruler Company; *Postage sticker:* me & my BIG ideas; *Mini postcard:* K & Company; *Metal:* Scrap Metal, Once Upon a Scribble; *Metal frame and shaped clip:* Making Memories; *Pewter sticker:* Magenta; *Watch charm:* The Card Connection; *Fibers:* Fibers By The Yard, On The Surface and DMC; *Stamping ink:* ColorBox, Clearsnap; Hero Arts; StazOn, Tsukineko; *Label maker:* Dymo.

Figure 3. Send patterned paper through your Dymo label maker for a customized look. *Page by Heather Uppencamp.* **Supplies** *Patterned paper and patterned vellum:* Chatterbox; *Vellum:* Chatterbox and Pebbles Inc.; *Mesh:* Maruyama, Magenta; *Rubber stamps:* Inkadinkado; *Stamping ink:* Hero Arts; *Heart-shaped clip and ribbon charm:* Making Memories; *Metal studs:* Scrapworks; *Label maker:* Dymo.

The journaling on the photo page reads:

"Mom, what was Grandma like?" Sometimes questions like this start a wonderful chain of thought , and a flood of memories. I remember...

...Gathering wild flowers to dry and dye for the amazing floral arrangements Mom used to make...

...Learning some basic tap dance steps from her just for fun...

...Following her finger as she pointed out how the notes went up and down in the hymn book we sang from on Sunday, and hearing her wonderful alto voice ...

...Learning to type from her, but never even getting close to her 50 words per minute...

...Visiting a sick neighbor with a wonderful, home-made meal and Mom's famous deep-dish apple pie ...

So Rachel, your grandmother was a wonderful person who left me with much more than memories, and I hope I am just a little bit like her.

Figure 4.
Use heavy-weight vellum in your Dymo label maker. *Card by Heather Uppencamp.*
Supplies *Patterned papers:* Rusty Pickle and Paper Pizazz; *Vellum:* Pebbles, Inc.; *Chalk:* Craf-T Products; *Label maker:* Dymo.

TINY EYELET TIP

I recently purchased some tiny ¹⁄₁₆" eyelets and was having trouble holding on to them long enough to set them. My fingers were too big; the tweezers were too big. Then I tried using a pushpin. It worked!

I was able to grasp the plastic end easily, and the pin fit into the eyelet perfectly. I positioned the pin where I wanted the eyelet to go and placed my entire page on a corkboard. I then pushed the pin through the paper and pushed the eyelet down the shaft of the pin, right into the hole where I could set it. This method has saved me both time and stress!

—Shannon Cleary, Riverside, RI

Embellished Pewter Accents

Although metal embellishments accentuate a layout beautifully "as is," you can customize them for a different look. Here are three techniques to try:

❶ Use a metallic leafing pen to highlight areas of the design (Figure 5). Draw over the areas you want to emphasize.

❷ Use a pigment inkpad and embossing powder to alter the color and surface texture of the metal (Figure 6). Generously apply the ink to the metal, then blot lightly with a tissue. Sprinkle clear embossing powder on the piece, tap off the excess and heat. *Tip:* For more color variation, apply two coordinating ink colors.

❸ Color the accent with glass paint applied with a paintbrush (Figure 7). Here I used Pebeo's Vetrea 160 (available at craft and art supply stores). For a more translucent look, thin the paint with a little water. Dry with a heat gun.

—*Marie-Ève Trudeau, Magenta*

Figure 5. Highlight portions of a metal accent with a metallic leafing pen. *Samples by Marie-Ève Trudeau for Magenta.* **Supplies** *Pewter sticker, metallic paper and patterned paper:* Magenta; *Gold leafing pen:* Krylon.

Figure 6. Customize a metal accent with stamping ink and embossing powder. *Samples by Marie-Ève Trudeau for Magenta.* **Supplies** *Pewter stickers and vellum:* Magenta; *Stamping ink:* ColorBox, Clearsnap; *Embossing powder:* Top Boss, Clearsnap; *Other:* Fibers.

Figure 7. Use glass paint to color a metal accent. *Samples by Marie-Ève Trudeau for Magenta.* **Supplies** *Pewter sticker, tag and cardboard tile:* Magenta; *Stamping ink:* ColorBox, Clearsnap; *Paint:* Vetrea 160, Pebeo; *Other:* Mulberry paper, fibers and pens. *Idea to note:* To raise the center section of her pewter sticker, Marie-Ève cut the section out, backed it with a thin cardboard tile, then reassembled the section on her tag.

our readers'
Best Photo Tips

Sharpen your skills— and pick up a reminder or two

Okay, I'll admit it—I'm not a great photographer. As I sift through photos looking for a subject to scrapbook, I'm reminded once again of a weakness—I don't have a knack for taking fantastic photos that draw the eye. How can I get those great shots? And how can I make the photos I've got work?

Like any other art form, photography takes practice to get better. I know I can save time and trouble if I listen to recommendations from experienced photographers. Armed with these tips from CK readers, I'm ready to go out and practice until I'm perfect—or at least better!

by Marianne Madsen

in doubt?
take the shot

I almost didn't take this photo at the Japanese Gardens in Portland, Oregon. I was convinced that the streaking sunlight would not photograph well and almost walked away. My husband persuaded me to take the shot anyway, with these magical results!

—*Carrie Christenson, Fairview, OR*

When in doubt, take the shot!

use an unexpected
splash of color

A nice but not amazing nature scene carries more punch with a splash of bright color in a subject's clothing. My husband took this photo of me and my brother hiking in the mountains above Santa Barbara, California. Try to imagine what this photo would look like had I been wearing a brown shirt instead of red! Don't be afraid to have your subjects dress colorfully.

—*Dana Schafer Forti, Los Angeles, CA*

Add a splash of color to brighten your photos.

go back **home**

Revisit your childhood neighborhood and take pictures. When I was little, my friends and I played on the railroad tracks—not a safe place, but our way of being rebellious! I went back to those tracks recently and was surprised at how much they had changed. The railroad tracks now go under the street, and one side ends in a pile of gravel. I took these photos, realizing that these tracks were a part of my childhood that I wanted to remember.

—Lisa Zanchi, Louisville, KY

Revisit a spot that was meaningful in your past. Document the changes in your old neighborhood.

Capture your subject while he or she is engrossed in something else.

catch them **unaware**

Your subject doesn't always need to be looking at the camera. In this picture, my daughter, Adelaide, had been picking azalea blooms off my mother's bush and was admiring her treasures. I snapped a quick picture and caught her pleasure and wonder on film.

—Lee Anne Russell, Brownsville, TN

Glasses without non-glare coating can divert attention from the subject's face.

avoid
glass glare

Glare is a common problem when shooting pictures of people wearing glasses. As a photographer, here are three recommendations for avoiding glass glare.

1 Glasses with a non-glare (anti-reflective) coating greatly reduce the amount of glare. The extra expense could be worth the investment for the avid photographer and scrapbooker.

2 If the photo is important enough to merit it, it's not difficult to quickly remove lenses from glass frames before taking pictures. I've done this numerous times, and it eliminates all risk of glass glare.

The photo here is of a family who discovered that the father had inoperable brain tumors and only a few months to live. Their desire was to capture him as they knew him: with his glasses on. We removed the lenses and proceeded with the photo shoot, concentrating on capturing family

Remove the glass from the frames to avoid any risk of glare.

3 If you took a great photo but it includes glass glare, simple photo editing can help—especially if the eyes are still visible. These photos show the same picture before and after using Adobe Photoshop. I selected and darkened the areas that were lighter because of glare and increased the contrast.

The eyes provide the greatest source of emotion. While glass glare can be a problem, with these easy tips you can avoid or fix it.

—*Allison Orthner, Calgary, AB, Canada*

Use Adobe Photoshop to remove glare from a photo if the eyes are still visible.

change your
background

When I viewed my digital pictures from a friend's wedding, I was disappointed to find they had a distinct yellow tone. I tried adjusting the tint and changing the photos to black and white, but I still didn't like the results. I decided to try keeping my subject in color and making the background black and white. This subtle effect removed the yellow tint and kept the focus on my subject. Here's how I did it:

1 Select the entire photo with the rectangle mask tool. Copy and paste the photo to a new image.

2 Convert the original image to black and white, then copy the black-and-white layer on top of the new color image.

3 Set the transparency on the eraser tool to 50%. Use the eraser tool to "erase" the black-and-white subject and reveal the underlying color subject. Zoom in and use a small brush size to move carefully along the edges. Sweep the area a few times to ensure all skin tones are even.

4 Crop and resize the image.

—Shelly Stearns, Urbana, IL

Unhappy with the background tint? Want to keep the focus on your subject?

Change the background to black and white and leave the subject in color.

try a
new angle

Turn your camera slightly to catch your subject at a new angle. (If you forget, you can tilt your photo later with photo-editing software.)

I loved the expression of my neighbor's daughter in her first Holy Communion dress. Still, I thought I could improve the photo from good to great. I used the "Rotate Canvas -> Arbitrary" command in Adobe Photoshop to tilt the canvas about 15 degrees to the right. Then I used the Crop tool to select a rectangular area that included Caitlin. I changed the image to Grayscale and fluffed up the black-and-white contrast.

—Pam Nafziger, McDonald, PA

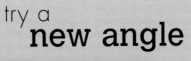
Make a good photograph . . .   great with a slight tilt.

enlarge
to 4" x 12"

I love the look of enlargements but find that I really miss the room to journal. Or, sometimes I don't need the whole photo to tell the story. While I could have a print enlarged to 8" x 12", that can be costly. Instead, I have a 4" x 12" print made from a regular 35mm negative at a quality mini-lab.

You'll get substantial cropping on the sides when you do this, so carefully consider the image you want to end up with. Look at the 4" x 6" image and use an index card or Post-it notes to mask off the area you want. If you can comfortably crop the photo to a 2" x 6" strip, you have a good candidate for a 4" x 12" print.

—Caroline Davis, Mentor, OH

Add visual punch to a "regular" photo by enlarging and cropping it. *Page by Caroline Davis.* **Supplies** *Patterned paper, vellum and tag:* SEI, Inc.; *Eyelet:* Making Memories; *Computer font:* CK Chemistry, "Fresh Fonts" CD, *Creating Keepsakes.*

hold your
breath

A great tip I picked up in a photography class? Just before you snap a photo, take a slight breath and hold it until after you've pressed the button. This will take the "shake" out of the action, and you'll stay as still as possible. This tip is especially helpful if you often experience slightly blurry or out-of-focus shots.

—Trudi Horner, West Lafayette, IN

try the
lens cap trick

When my son was a toddler, he was much more interested in running around than posing for photos. I took him outside one day for a photo session but couldn't get him to stand still.

In desperation, I threw the lens cap where I wanted him to stand. While he bent over to pick it up, I focused my camera. My son was so thrilled to get the lens cap that he had a huge smile on his face when he stood up. I got great results!

—Nicky Hurt, Mildenhall, England

Not all films are the same.
See what we discovered in our film test drive!

Agfa, Fuji, Kodak—these and others are the film brands you've purchased and used for years. While you may think all work equally well under different conditions, you're in for a surprise.

CK sent photographer Allison Landy on a "test drive" with different films. She shot pictures indoors and outdoors, in direct light, in shade, in window light and more. "I found definite differences in how the films performed," says Allison.

To see Allison's results and get her recommendations, check out "The Right Film," an exclusive online feature at *www.creatingkeepsakes.com/mag*.

Photos by Allison Landy

label your film

I keep address labels in my purse to put on my film before turning it in for developing. I stick an address label on each developing envelope as well. This is quicker than hand writing the envelope, and it's easier for the photo lab people to read. You can even make labels on your computer and number them to coincide with your notes of where and when you took the pictures.

—*Cynthia Heng, Enid, OK*

try this tape trick

Distraction is the key to keeping a toddler still long enough to take a good photo. One thing that works for me is to put a small loop of tape on my toddler's fingertip. The resulting expression of concentration makes a nice photo.

—*Terri Davenport, Toledo, OH*

date your photos

At the beginning of each roll of film, I take a photo of a sheet of paper with the month and year written on it. That way, I always know how old the kids are in the photos. This works especially well if I don't get to the photos right away.

—*Shobha George*
Lethbridge, AB, Canada

Editor's note: Taking a picture of a current calendar page works as well.

add a
sense of scale

On our visit to Southern Utah, we visited an out-of-the-way rock formation called "The Wave." The wind-eroded rock formations are so unusual in color and form that the view would have no idea of scale were it not for my husband, Mark, and our Springer spaniel, Sherpa, in the foreground.

Mark took a photo of me in a September snowstorm in Banff National Park in Alberta, Canada. Including a person in the shot gave scale and drama to the landscape, evoking an image of a lone person braving the harsh elements of nature. Without the person, the photo would have no clear subject, and the feeling of chilly winter would be diminished.

—*Dana Schafer Forti, Los Angeles, CA*

Include a person in a landscape photo to show scale.

Evoke an image of frail humanity in the midst of nature.

develop a system for
naming photos

I recently scanned my heritage photos so I could have them printed at a local lab. The default name assigned to each photo (such as "scan 0001.jpg") was meaningless, so I changed the file names to something more descriptive. For example, I named a 1931 photo of my father "1931_ChasBrooks.jpg" and a 1939 photo of my father and his siblings "1939_BrooksSiblings.jpg."

With the year at the beginning of the file name, the images sort chronologically. When I had the photos printed, the file names were printed on the back. The index print also had the file names below the thumbnails. Contact your photo lab to see if its printing system has any restrictions on file naming conventions.

—*Laura McGrover, Clearwater, FL*

meter your
subject's face

Don't have a handheld light meter? Use your in-camera meter to help filter out light manually. Simply bring your SLR camera up very closely to the subject's face and press the shutter button down halfway. Look inside the viewfinder to see what the in-camera meter reads (something like "5.6/250"). Step back, reposition yourself to get the angle you want, and manually set your camera for the reading from the in-camera meter.

—*Sherri Winstead Fayetteville, NC* ❤

selecting a

DIGITAL CAMERA

Discover our best finds – **under $300**!

CK editorial assistant Fred Brewer calls me "Ms. Techno Savvy," and I just have to laugh. I'm *really a* mom who loves to scrapbook pictures of her child. Why the association with technology? I "went digital" two years ago, and my first *Creating Keepsakes* article was in the Computer Corner column. Guess that makes me a scrapbooking mom who understands that technology can be a scrapbooker's best friend!

text by
RACHEL THOMAE

article design by
BECKY HIGGINS

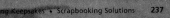

CHOOSING MUST-HAVES

I translate the wish list into digital camera terms, then make a chart to help me decide which cameras will suit my scrapbooking friends' needs. Here's what I include on the chart:

MEGAPIXELS (MP)

3MP Cameras: Print quality 4" x 6", 5" x 7" and 8" x 10" photographs

4MP and 5MP Cameras: Print quality photographs that are up to 24" x 36" in print format. Larger file sizes may produce sharper image quality on larger prints. Larger file sizes allow for more computer touch-ups (including cropping) without losing print quality.

READING MY MAIL

Since I've been dubbed "Ms. Techno Savvy," my co-workers in the CK office forward technology questions to me. Lately, I've received several letters like this one:

"I really want to go digital, but I'm afraid to spend my money on something that may not suit my needs. I'm a basic point-and-shoot kind of person. What should I look for? I'm so confused by terms such as 'pixels,' 'zoom' and 'memory size.' How much should I pay for a good quality, middle-of-the-road digital camera? I need suggestions on what to buy for a reasonable price." — Shannon Kellogg, Cottage Grove, WI

For help coming up with recommendations, I call the girls in my Friday night scrapbooking group and ask what they'd like in their "dream" digital camera. My friend Lisa says, "I want good quality photographs. And I want to be able to zoom in on my daughter's face."

Angela adds, "My sister's digital camera is too complicated, and I hate reading manuals. I want a digital camera that I can just take out of the box and start using! And I want to be able to put it in my purse." Karen tells me she wants a camera for less than $300.

ZOOM

2x Optical Zoom
Zoom in from 8 feet away

3x Optical Zoom
Zoom in from 10 feet away

4x Optical Zoom
Zoom in from 15 feet away

6x Optical Zoom
Zoom in from 25 feet away

8x Optical Zoom
Zoom in from 35 feet away